Do Nothing

The Simple Principles of Jesus
Accomplish Anything

~~HUSTLE~~

~~TRY HARDER~~

~~EARN IT~~

DO NOTHING

JONATHAN COTTRELL

NASHVILLE

NEW YORK • LONDON • MELBOURNE • VANCOUVER

Do Nothing

The Simple Principles of Jesus to Accomplish Anything

© 2022 Jonathan Cottrell

Published in New York, New York, by Morgan James Publishing. Morgan James is a trademark of Morgan James, LLC. www.MorganJamesPublishing.com

Proudly distributed by Ingram Publisher Services.

A **FREE** ebook edition is available for you
or a friend with the purchase of this print book.

CLEARLY SIGN YOUR NAME ABOVE

Instructions to claim your free ebook edition:
1. Visit MorganJamesBOGO.com
2. Sign your name CLEARLY in the space above
3. Complete the form and submit a photo of this entire page
4. You or your friend can download the ebook to your preferred device

ISBN 9781631957840 paperback
ISBN 9781631957857 ebook
Library of Congress Control Number:
2021947649

Cover Design by:
Chris Treccani
www.3dogcreative.net

Interior Design by:
Christopher Kirk
www.GFSstudio.com

Morgan James is a proud partner of Habitat for Humanity Peninsula and Greater Williamsburg. Partners in building since 2006.

Get involved today! Visit MorganJamesPublishing.com/giving-back

To Frank Viola,
a brother

CONTENTS

HOW DO I WORK WITH JESUS?

WHAT IS GOD'S PLAN FOR ME?

EVERYTHING THAT REMAINS

INTRODUCTION

This book shouldn't exist. Even a quick glance at the title should reek of irony. How does an author writing about doing nothing publish something? Snap judgment or jeers would not be misplaced. Count me as surprised as anyone.

Before writing this, I was halfway finished writing another much longer and very different book. In fact, I already had more pages written in that manuscript than the number I've published here. The work was accelerating, and my goal was within reach. But something changed.

After months of pages flowing as quickly as I could type them, all my momentum died. It was as though I had been sailing on the open seas, my mast tall and strong, with the wind at my back and my destination in sight. The land I would call "Finished" was but a small distance ahead of me, my anticipation building. And then, there was nothing. The wind suddenly stopped. My journey came to a standstill.

As the perceived captain of this ship, I had a choice. When writing a book, it's more about the science of discipline and willpower than it is art alone. I very well *could* have continued forward, powered by my own strength. I could have pulled out the paddles, as it were, and rowed ahead until my feet finally touched the ground and I could call the journey complete.

Or, I had another option.

Typically, I would have diagnosed my slow progress as an unfortunate bout of writer's block. But after months of absolutely no wind in my so-called sails—utter quiet, zero new ideas, even mental resistance to just sitting down and writing it—I prayed. "What are You doing, Jesus?"

There, amid the frustrating calm, my Lord responded with a clear word, but without immediate clarity as to why He was delivering it: "Wait."

For those who find themselves anything like me, waiting is not quite my cup of tea. Even at that, I'm being generous. I *hate* waiting. Impatience is something of a character trait that I try to spin as a good thing. Rather than rightly call it a struggle, in the legendary words of Tom Cruise in *Top Gun*, I prefer to say that "I feel the need, the need for speed."

But here I found myself, smack dab in the middle of completing my first book, desiring nothing more than to finish it, and God encouraged me to pause. In fact, even as I write this, I'm not entirely sure if He has told me to pause or stop altogether. Maybe that's something I'll find out later, maybe not. I can only recommunicate what He communicated to me as plainly as I heard it. "Wait."

Why did He do that? Why did He care? Why did He seemingly provide all this prior momentum before stopping me on my way? Because He had this little book planned, instead. Please realize that I am not suggesting every word of this work to be inspired by God. Certainly not. I am sure readers will find enough of me in this book to identify its failings. I am wildly imperfect, but I am grateful that He will use me, as much as He supplies me with His grace to do so.

I have heard other stories like mine, but I had never experienced it so directly. One of my dear friends, Chad, comes to mind. Near the end of his doctoral studies, when writing the very last paper he needed to receive the degree he had worked toward for six years, he felt a gentle nudge within his spirit. "You've learned all you needed to. You're done."

On Chad's pursuit to become a pastor at his local church, it was on this same course of theological and ministry education that the Lord introduced him to how the early Christians understood what it meant to *be* the church. As a result, Chad no longer agreed with what he was studying to do vocationally. Rather than resist the Lord as I may have in a similar circumstance, Chad submitted his will to Christ. He did not question God. He did not try to make a deal. He just didn't turn in his final paper. After years of study and investment, Chad never received his doctorate, choosing instead to claim that the Lord and His ways were knowledge enough for him. What obedience.

My personal surprise with this effort doesn't begin with the tale of how I was to finish another book first, either. As a many-time entrepreneur and self-described "serial starter," *Do Nothing* is not the type of title I would run toward on the shelves. Honestly, I'm quite impressed that anyone has decided to pick up this book to begin with because this definitely isn't the popular message of today. *Work hard. Hustle. Earn it. Try harder. Don't stop. Keep going. Make it happen.* Modern culture inundates us with quips and mantras that indoctrinate us to our seemingly always insufficient action. This is just as true within the church.

So here I found myself, halfway done with something else and awaiting further instruction. While I felt God had catalyzed the work of my freshman book, He had also paused it. We see stories like this throughout scripture, too. For example, the Israelites were led by God out of Egypt and through the Red Sea, but eventually God said He would not proceed forward with them into the Promised Land. Moses intercedes. "If Your presence will not go with me, do not bring us up from here. For how shall it be known that I have found favor in Your sight, I and Your people? Is it not in Your going with us, so that we are distinct, I and Your people, from every other people on the face of the Earth" (Exodus 33:15-16)?

While we always have the presence of God with us—better yet, inside us—we are too often willing to march forward without the undeniable distinction of His presence in what we do. *I won't go anywhere without Your presence, Lord.* Is that our attitude? Or are we more inclined to shrug our shoulders in concession, moving ahead of God's Spirit? I fear I too many times do the latter. We can learn from Moses.

The Lord so often calls us to pause with Him, yet we do everything we can to keep pushing ahead, trudging forward with Him at our backs. We're His followers, but we try to drag Him along with us, leading the way ourselves. How can God prepare good works for us to walk in if He does not go before us, paving our steps forward? Returning to my original analogy, we incline ourselves to pull out the paddles—or build a motor—and try to reach our intended destinations by our independent strength and devices. Despite what we may believe, our ingenuity and hard work alone never lead to genuine works of God.

Ultimately, I listened, pausing the book I had begun. What better way for the Lord to illustrate the principle of His most necessary presence both in—and to—me? Jesus knows I need such lessons. It is appropriate that I, a serial starter, had to stop something altogether before the Lord could begin what He wanted to do.

Finally, after months of waiting, I felt the Lord's wind again fill my sails, only pointed to a new destination this time. He gently prodded me forward in writing this book,

Do Nothing, before I could write anything else. Without His urging, I am done trying to complete anything on my own.

There's more. Were sailing to a whole new destination not enough, something came to afflict me after finishing just one chapter of this book. Two weeks into writing, my hand began tremoring one evening and all energy felt sapped from my body. Over the coming weeks, severe fatigue sank in as well. I cannot tell anyone what my ailments were as my symptoms have since passed, but I did everything I could to figure out what it was that affected me. That answer never came directly, even after neurologist visits, blood work, MRIs, dietary changes, and more.

Looking back, I now suspect that it was through my momentary challenge that the Lord desired to complete this specific work. He did not wish for me to rely on my strength and willpower, but to grow so weak that only the endurance of God could help me author this. Even though I do not believe He directly caused my affliction, sometimes we each need a thorn in our flesh (2 Corinthians 12:7-9).

All this introduction is to say that, quite literally, this book finally finds itself in readers' hands as a testimony not of me or my abilities, but of Christ Jesus and His supreme power. I pray it is a resolute testimony that declares the truth of our very existence, that "With man this is impossible, but with God all things are possible" (Matthew 19:26). Yes, many other books have been written by men and women over the centuries. But in reality, there is one Author alone who makes any work possible. While I pray that the Lord may uncover more of Himself and His ways through these humble words, I cannot take a single ounce of credit if that happens. All honor and glory belong to Him alone.

Counting myself among such ranks, I commit this book to the doers, the workers, the hustlers, the strivers, the builders, the earners, the starters, the producers, and the achievers. As well intentioned as we each may have felt in our hard work and effort, let us look with spiritual eyes upon the output of our hands to see what will stand everlasting. "Unless the Lord builds the house, they labor in vain who build it" (Psalm 127:1). I always used to recite that Psalm, I just rarely applied it to my daily life. Maybe I understand it a little better now. Maybe.

Whatever the case, by God's astounding grace, I am confident of this—I can do nothing apart from Christ. Just… nothing. In this personal revelation, I can also declare that something of genuine value has been accomplished. For inasmuch as this book shouldn't exist, it does. Consider it my gift to everyone it may touch, made possible solely by Him.

Together, let us now join Jesus in a vineyard as He shares the principles to accomplishing absolutely anything, anywhere, anytime. It may surprise us.

My precious Jesus, please supply me. I cannot think any thought worth thinking or type any word worth typing without You, for I am undeniably weak and entirely incapable without You. I place this work into Your hands as much as I know how to do so, assured that any measure of beauty or usefulness that may be realized in these humble pages can only be attributed to You and Your eternal grace. Amen.

WHAT CAN I DO?

"...apart from Me, you can do nothing."
John 15:5

SELF-MADE TOWERS

He disgusted me. Though we never exchanged a single word of conversation, I quickly gathered every piece of knowledge I needed to pass my silent judgment.

Contrary to my personal opinion, I'm sure others admired this man a great deal. As he stepped out of his pricey, freshly waxed sports car, he undeniably appeared impressive. At nearly six-and-a-half feet tall, built like an athlete at the top of his game, he boasted all the makings of a model you might see on the cover of *GQ* or another popular men's fashion magazine. His suit was sharp, tailored. His hair looked like it had just been cut and meticulously sculpted. His walk oozed confidence. Clearly, he had done well for himself.

Working as a valet at the time, he left his driver side door ajar for scrawny, 19-year-old me to quickly hop in and park his V12 sports car. I cheerily made my way toward his expensive vehicle, eager to get behind the wheel. But as he quietly turned his broad shoulders toward the country club where I worked, it was then that I saw his license plate. Though just a single hyphenated word, it spoke volumes. Centered on the tailgate of his black convertible, the plate read: SLFMADE.

"Gross," I immediately thought to myself. I wouldn't be surprised if I even cringed, physically displaying my repugnance.

Raised in the church over my youth and considering myself in love with Jesus, I couldn't fathom how someone could develop such a blatant disregard of the Divine. Did this man not realize he had been created by God? Did he not know how pompous this "self-made" inscription actually made him look, regardless of his otherwise impeccable appearances? Did he not understand that a haughty spirit comes before the fall (Proverbs 16:18)? My palpable contempt continued for several minutes, distinct enough that it left a long-lasting impression.

It only took me sixteen years to reconsider my response. The flippant statement made on that license plate still burdens me. but the gentlemen whose name I never learned is no longer the object of my disgust. Instead, I am grieved by my own self-righteous judgment and condemnation of him. I was wildly, terribly wrong.

In fact, the truth is even more severe: *I am this man.* Though I do not drive his luxury car or wear his designer suits, at least a little bit of him resides in me. To be exact,

I believe pieces of him can be discovered in most humans today. Yes, that includes Christians. In this regard, the Irish novelist Marian Keyes struck a painful chord in her observation, "The things we dislike most in others are the characteristics we like least in ourselves."

Don't misunderstand me. As followers of Jesus, I'm certain we all understand that we are not the Creator of ourselves, reserving that title for God alone. We would probably—hopefully—stop short of attaching ourselves to arrogant labels that so garishly assert what we have made by our own strength. Still, despite our basic knowledge of the true Maker, who do we genuinely believe is the inventor of our thinking and abilities? Who do we think has formed our families and our experiences? Who has gained the credit for placing and promoting us in our careers? Who is the author cited with our accomplishments? Do we reserve these non-Creator titles for Jesus, or have we accepted them as ours?

Though I hate admitting it, like this successful man I encountered years ago, I have regularly believed that my appearances and achievements are the result of my own commitment and hard work. I have quietly tallied my efforts against the effort of others, even in ministry, to artificially bolster my self-esteem. In other words, I too have preposterously considered most of my life to be "self-made."

Granted, we may not consciously realize what we are doing. I didn't. But just because we are unaware of our motives doesn't make us any less culpable.

Thank Jesus for His astounding grace. Though my heart has been slower than my mind to grasp this fundamental truth, God has been merciful to me, helping me become painfully aware of my profound misunderstandings. That man was but one of many mirrors the Lord has kindly sent me so that can I more fully see the ungodly shape and color of my own flesh. In fact, God will reflect this same mercy to anyone who gazes with spiritual eyes upon Christ's perfect form and radiance.

Though the man I encountered that day wrongly supposed that he had constructed his own six-foot, six-inch tower of self on his own, it is clear to me now that I have just as regularly ventured to create numerous self-made monuments. Like those who have come before us, we may subtly think, "Come, let us make a name for ourselves" erecting our own idolatrous towers of Babel in the process (Genesis 11:4). We so often try to impress the world using our talent and inventiveness rather than building according to the wise plans of our great Architect (Genesis 11:3; Hebrews 11:10).

Look around the world today and we will agree that humankind has come to fully rely upon its own skills and innovation, apparently making giant leaps in the process. Unfortunately, we have confused our constructive capabilities to infer that we can do something apart from Christ. We try to attain something, rather than obtain that which Jesus has freely given us. We seek to change our life, rather than exchanging it for the Life. We do rather than let the Lord undo us. Quite simply, we fall short (Romans 3:23).

Just because we *could* do something does not automatically mean that we *should* do something. Frequently, I have mistaken my God-given abilities to construe that, as a result, I must do something. I have even labeled these verbs the very calling of Jesus—to do, to create, to build, to make, to produce, to go, and so on. Inasmuch as these tasks contain truth to which we should all respond in our varied walks of faith, they are not those we should look to first when grasping the calling we have each received (Romans 8:28). They have nothing to do with our worth as God's image-bearers (Genesis 1:27).

Our worth was instilled into each of us by our magnificent Maker before we ever did anything. Despite anything we have done, will do, or ever can do, God loves us beyond all measure or superlative description. There are no human words excessive enough to explain the measurement of God's incomparable value and intimate love for us (Ephesians 1:17-19). Though the vernacular may strike us as too familiar, cliché, even boring in Christian circles, the mind-bending, life-changing, and ground-shaking reality remains: God unconditionally loves us with fierce and reckless abandon. Even as our love of God may waver or go silent, His remains steadfast, resounding, and limitless (Psalm 36:5; 57:10; 86:15; 89:14, 33; 100:5; 108:4; 1 John 4:19).

As a result, we no longer need to apply labels to and identify ourselves by our accomplishments. We would be wise to set aside our personal work having anything whatsoever to do with our worth in life. When we do this, we may finally reach the point in our adventures of faith where we are ready to receive the real job assignment of every Christian. The King of the universe assuredly has something for each of us to do, but it will sound, look, and feel quite unlike anything we have ever done before. It will not be work in the traditional sense of the word. In fact, it will have absolutely nothing to do with what is self-made. Zip. Zero. Zilch.

Unfortunately, the Lord's work will even seem contrary to that which much of the church describes as our individual responsibility. Whether this type of Christian obligation is taught openly from the pulpit or it remains a masked burden of expectation and judgment hung around the neck of every believer within their respective community, the responsibility the Lord has placed upon us is far easier and worlds lighter than we could ever imagine on our own (Matthew 11:30). Whatever we may think we know of God's calling, it pales in comparison to the utter simplicity of it (2 Corinthians 11:3, NASB).

When we stop basing our self-worth and personal value on what we have made of, by, and for ourselves, we should readily discover a job description to be quite helpful in explaining what it is we are really supposed to do. After all, if we accept the wrong job description, how can we set out to do the right work? We can't.

Unwittingly, this is precisely what we have done. In our elevation of our individual abilities, personal achievements, and esteem-boosting titles, we have each errored at some point in trying to perform spiritual work that we have neither the God-given responsibility or authority to carry out (Matthew 8:5-10). Though we have all been chosen as people who will follow the Name above every name, we have too commonly named ourselves the Heads, Directors, and Leaders of so-called kingdom endeavors, routinely setting out to accomplish work that fails to serve the ultimate intentions of God (Matthew 23:8-12).

Yes, our skyrises of self keep ascending, brick by brick; but every one of them must be demolished if we desire for God's highest plans to be assembled among us, stone by stone (Genesis 11:3; 1 Peter 2:4-5). Though we may often find ourselves inspired by the towers of men, God is building something altogether different and indestructible (Psalm 127:1; Matthew 16:18). It is not self-made, it is Christ-made (John 1:1-3).

In response, it is here and now that we are each invited to surrender our individual misconceptions and inaccurate descriptions of duty so that we might accept the assignment that Jesus has prepared for us to accomplish in Him. It is the job we were destined for before the foundations of the world, written in the heavenlies, outside of time itself. It is our real responsibility.

Are we ready for our assignment?

EVERY CHRISTIAN'S JOB

As followers of Christ, our job description is simple: Do nothing.

Everyone read that correctly. Nothing. As in, *nothing*. Full stop.

Let those two words sink into our minds and hearts. Breathe them in. Say it out loud if it helps, "My job is to do nothing."

How can this be? Impossible. Not true. As any Bible-believing Christian, we are bound to consider these responses while entertaining such a sensational claim—though it must not come as too great a surprise given this book's title.

Regardless of anyone's particular reaction, though, it is true. Walking in a vineyard soon before His crucifixion, Jesus teaches His disciples, "I am the Vine; you are the branches. Whoever abides in Me and I in him, he it is that bears much fruit, for apart from Me you can *do nothing*" (John 15:5).

Some will still consider this job description too structureless, even inaccurate, based on the contextual words of Christ. True, thorough exegesis of this Bible verse has led many to describe every Christian's job as something quite different than "do nothing." With even a quick glance at most commentaries, we would find that many theologians and fellow ministers in Christ have reached very different conclusions around this specific passage.

Asked the question through the lens of this scripture alone, many Christians summarize our responsibility as *abiding*. Looking at the text, this is plain to see and should be truth every disciple agrees is an effort we should make. We are called to abide. We will consider what it means to restfully abide in later chapters, because Jesus said it and our lives will be well served as we learn how to do exactly this, without question.

Still, others extrapolate from this passage that the job of every Christian is *bearing fruit*. Yes, the theme of fruitfulness runs throughout the entirety of scripture, right from the beginning in Genesis 1, all the way to its conclusion in Revelation 22. God intends for us to bear fruit as we abide in Him, our Vine and Tree of Life (Matthew 7:17-19; 13:23; Galatians 5:22-23; Colossians 1:9-10). Good fruit is something every Christian should hope to, expect to, and will bear, for our Lord promised so as He gave this farewell discourse to His disciples.

Considering the Bible as a whole, many Christians will summarize our mission using different language altogether, saying we are to *love God and love people*, or *serve the Lord*, or *make disciples*, and so on (Matthew 22:37-40; 28:18-20; John 12:26). Every one of these descriptions carry weight and should be considered when fully reflecting upon the call of all believers in Jesus Christ, because they are biblical and, therefore, inspired by God (2 Timothy 3:16).

All this is to say: we need not argue with these alternative Christian job descriptions. God intends for us to abide in Christ, bear fruit, love people, serve Him, make disciples, and more.

However, while none of these ideas are wrong in and of themselves, as with seemingly any human endeavor, such conclusions emphasize where we too frequently look for our worth—in doing something. Therefore, the error in these substitute definitions lies not in our conclusions, but in our emphases. Culture's focus—and by osmosis, our focus—is on doing. *What do you do? What have you been doing? What are you doing? What will you be doing this weekend?* So much doing.

Christ's assignment is very different: do nothing. Our shoulders may become tense at the mere thought of this perceived idleness. We are not alone, either. Personally, I am wildly uncomfortable with the idea. This declaration of Christ runs counter to every bone in my body, every intuition of my mind, and every system of this world. "But I must do something," I contend. "God calls me to it." Does He, though?

Jesus never calls us to a way that He did not walk in perfectly Himself. As He professes, "Truly, truly, I say to you, the Son can *do nothing* of His own accord" (John 5:19). If we did not understand Him the first time, the Son of God drives home His point even more plainly just moments later. "I can *do nothing* on My own" (John 5:30).

Coming from the lips of the Word who spoke all things into creation, we should not glaze over these statements so quickly. Unfortunately, this aspect of Christ's life remains one rarely taught today. Regardless, the truth remains— Jesus lived in the exact same way that we are called to live. He recognized that He could do nothing except by the residing, indwelling life and power of His Father. We can do nothing apart from Jesus now just as He could do nothing apart from God the Father then.

Imagine for just a moment how often Jesus might have felt the urge to resist this way of existence. Waiting thirty years for your life's high calling to begin requires no small amount of patience. Hebrews explains as much, teaching that Jesus was "tempted in every respect as we are" (Hebrews 4:15). Did that temptation not also include the frequent impulse to do something that He wanted rather than His Father wanted? I imagine so.

Thankfully, Jesus always submitted His will to the Father, even unto death (Luke 22:42). But make no mistake about it, we serve a King who sympathizes with us

(Hebrews 4:15). Even when it comes to our weak, spiritually misplaced efforts to do something on our own—as good, purposeful, and righteous as those things may often seem to us—Jesus understands. He gets it. Our God who took on flesh was just as tempted to do something on His own as we might regularly feel to do something on ours.

It only requires a limited reading of the Bible to know there is much more to say about our calling as Christians than these two words alone. But in this time of so much human effort, I believe doing nothing is the responsibility we must remember and practice more than ever. We are such busy, complicating beings—always planning, working, striving, building. This is the age of hustle…and we say that as though it is a good thing.

I am not here to argue that there is no work to be done or no "thing" to do. Honestly, I have written this to solidify the understanding for myself as much as anybody else. We should each take the time necessary to evaluate and rethink what we continue doing.

Yes, there is great good to be found in the spirit of those *willing* to work for the Lord, but we err in how much we let our doing proceed what Jesus is doing. We originate the work rather than allowing Him to originate it. Though we may not readily admit it, our doing often lacks faith that He is doing something. Worse, we regularly miss what He is doing altogether, wrongly believing it is mostly—or entirely—up to us. Nothing could be further from the truth. God is at work!

Having been shaken, stirred, and ultimately distracted by an enticing cocktail of the culture, the enemy, and yes, even our own flesh, let us come to readily believing and fully acknowledging that our job is first discovered in these two uncomplicated, yet revolutionary words: Do nothing. Nothing is the training ground for the something that God will have us do as we rest in the authoring and finishing work of Jesus Christ. As we wholly believe and completely surrender to the truth that we are responsible for doing nothing apart from Him, finally, something will begin to get done.

CRUCIFIED CAN-DOS

As we have each read, prayed through, and reflected upon Christ's pronouncement from John 15:5, we will eventually discover a miracle of God's work occurring within us. At last, we may accept our first job assignment as Christians—this doing nothing which Jesus so plainly declared. Frustratingly, it is here that many of us will likely uncover our flesh misleading us once again.

Having heard the passage of the Vine and the branches regularly taught in my youth, I thought I understood what was being laid out by Christ. But as I learn to undertake the simple job that has been divinely assigned to me, the exact words of Jesus challenge me to my core. Even up until recently, I have found myself often repeating, "I *must* do nothing." But this declaration misses the point of what Jesus stated, word for word.

Christ does not teach us, "You can do something, but instead, I tell you to do nothing." He doesn't even say, "You must do nothing." No. In His spiritual picture of the Vine and its branches, Jesus proclaims through scripture, "apart from Me, you *can* do nothing" (John 15:5).

In confession from my personal experience, I admit that the skeptic in me works overtime to resist such wild claims. *I am capable. Look at all I have done on my own. Of course I can do something, just watch me.* But the truth stands, absolute and unshakable. I cannot do anything. Nobody can. If there is one imperative thing we "must" do, it is carrying every one of our can-do beliefs to the cross so that they might be crucified. Our abilities must die to become inabilities. *I am unable.* Our somethings must die to become nothings. *I have done nothing on my own.* Our can-dos must die to become cannots. *I cannot do anything.*

In the light of God's explicit words, our faith in His power does not begin with believing that Jesus exclusively seeks to accomplish big, impossible work with us. Instead, the gift of our faith begins where we realize Christ is the One because of Whom, through Whom, and in Whom we are capable of carrying out even the smallest, slightest, seemingly doable actions of every day. Actions like waking, eating, moving, and even breathing would not be possible apart from Him. The apostle Paul declared as much to the men of Athens, hoping to persuade them. He reveals, "[God] is actually not far from each one of us, for 'In Him we live and move and have our being'" (Acts 17:22-31).

Consider, what has given us the ability to read these very words? If we claim it is our intelligence and prior diligence in learning how to read, then what first gave us the ability to see these words or any words before them? If we believe our eyesight is due to our parents' imparted genetics, then what is it that gave them their ability to reproduce, thereby leading to our healthy birth and vision? Following this old but straightforward trail of thought, eventually we will all arrive at the crossroads of our very existence. We can either travel down a twisted path—thinking we are capable, self-made controllers who can move without God—or we can journey with the living Jesus, convinced that we cannot take one step forward without Him. For what is it that separates us from someone else who does not have use of even the most basic human capacities— the biological abilities that afford us physical life and consciousness at this very moment?

As we behold these words with our eyes, understand them with our minds, and enjoy the breath that God has afforded each one of us, we should become assured that everything we have—absolutely everything—is nothing more than a result of divine providence (Genesis 2:7). Not only can we do nothing, but we would *be* nothing were it not for Jesus. John the Baptist proclaims similarly to his disciples, "A person cannot receive even one thing unless it is given him from heaven" (John 3:27).

In the Christian classic, *The Practice of God's Presence*, a seventeenth-century monk named Brother Lawrence beautifully conveys this spiritual reality with equal certainty. Though we so regularly take our little abilities for granted, our ancient brother did not. "Whenever [Lawrence] considered doing some good deed, he always consulted God about it, saying, 'Lord, I will never be able to do that if You don't help me.' Immediately he would be given more than enough strength."

This brother monastically exercised the understanding of his inability well beyond common practice, articulating, "I flip my little omelet in the frying pan for the love of God, and when it's done, if I have nothing to do, I prostrate myself on the floor and adore my God who gave me the grace to do it, after which I get up happier than a king."

While I will admit again that every fiber of my flesh hunts for the loopholes to resist fundamental principles like my inability to cook a few cracked eggs, the Spirit of God confirms this truth. Let us hear Him whisper the eternal words of Jesus within us even now. "Apart from Me, you can do nothing." It's time to cement His words in our minds, etch them upon our hearts, and stop believing we are so capable of something on our own. We are wildly, ridiculously, unfathomably incapable.

Held together by Christ in this very second, it is in such reflective moments that the eyes of our hearts may finally open to the reality of Reality itself (Colossians 1:17). Every ounce of energy we call our own is solely present within us because it is His own and He has filled us with it. Just as scripture proclaims, "He is the Fullness that fills all in all"

(Ephesians 1:23). Either we believe that Christ is All, or we do not (Colossians 3:11).

The apostle Paul understood this wholly and lived his new life in Christ accordingly. In Colossians, he writes, "For this I toil, struggling with all His energy that He powerfully works within me" (Colossians 1:29). Our bondservant brother understood that work needed to be done, without question. But most importantly, Paul knew that the only way this work could be accomplished was by the energy that God was presently supplying him. This was work that God needed to do and Paul could not. Thankfully, God continues that work today in each one of us, powerfully speaking and supplying His energy to us in this very moment.

As A.W. Tozer agrees in *The Pursuit of God*, "The word of God is the breath of God filling the world with living potentiality. The Voice of God is the most powerful force in nature, indeed the only force in nature, for all energy is here only because the power-filled Word is being spoken."

What can we possibly expect or reasonably believe to accomplish without Christ in the first place? Whatever of those ideas may remain, let every one of them go. They are not God's ideas. May we place piercing nails into the resilient hands and racing legs of our so-called strength. For inasmuch as God wants us to do nothing apart from Him, we just as much cannot do something—or anything, for that matter—apart from Him.

PORTRAITS OF THE CHURCH

I n an uncontrollable, flailing fit, our logical reason may throw one last tantrum, trying to contest our inability. Mine certainly does. We fling a final argument into the arena of debate, "No, just 'apart from' Christ we can do nothing, but *in* Him, we still must do something." Pride is on the prowl, doing everything it can to survive. I am as guilty as anyone.

Fortunately, the Bible doesn't just offer us words to help us understand this truth—it's a picture book, too. Since the beginning, the Word of God has been painting with magnificent strokes to reveal life, light, color, and form as we know it. Similarly, the Spirit of God has inspired numerous portraits of meaning and substance throughout scripture, employing vivid imagery to help the church grapple with her inability apart from Christ.

Let us rethink what we can do one last time by analyzing the same picture that Jesus painted for us—a vine. If we have never personally visited a vineyard, imagining an ordinary fruit tree will suffice instead. While we may at first describe a branch's job as abiding in the vine or trunk, a truth to which we have already agreed, consider what such branches are doing by their own strength as they abide.

In its beautiful foliage which it did not create and splendid fruit which it did not invent, is it a branch's job to do something, or is it the source of that branch's life to feed it the necessary nutrients and remain firmly planted? Can a branch think and work and strive and push itself to grow something? Have we ever seen a branch walking around, cleverly determining how to develop more fruit and serve others through its produce?

As much as these ideas may seem comical when put so plainly, we should witness it for ourselves if necessary. Detach a healthy nearby branch to see how quickly its color fades and its fruit withers. The strength to abide is not found in the fortitude of a branch, but in the rootedness of its vine. Fruit-bearing, too, cannot be done by a branch, but purely by the root. Fortunately for us, we abide not only in the Vine but in the Root of David (Isaiah 11:1; Revelation 5:5).

My dad, Dave, frequently employs another analogy when speaking about a Christian's ability. Unlike fruit, it is not discovered at ground level, but in the skies. As we gaze upon the moon from Earth's surface at night, it appears that it provides a significant source of light. Especially on eve-nings we encounter a full moon, the light this otherwise gray mass affords our blue planet makes quite a difference in the dark. But as my dad wisely pointed out to me while I looked up at it many nights by his side, the moon supplies no light of its own. In his exact words, "It's just a big, dead rock."

My dad is right. Our planet's moon emits no light, and yet, in the darkness, it shines. Its job, indeed its very nature is to reflect the source of all light that we have in our solar system by virtue of its position to the sun. The moon was made to glorify the sun, just as one aspect of humanity's purpose is to glorify the Light of the world, Jesus Christ. The darkness cannot overtake God's Light, whether direct or reflected (John 1:5).

In fact, were we to inspect each spiritual image that God's word uses to paint pictures of the church's respon-sibility in Christ, we would discover not one prophetic representation placing the responsibility upon our doing something without Jesus. Let us take a quick refresher course on the familiar images used throughout scripture to commonly portray the church.

We are living stones, being built together as God's house (Ephesians 2:22). What can stones do on their own, let alone as an unfinished pile of rocks? Yet the truth remains, even the rocks would cry out His praise were we not to do so (Luke 19:40).

We are a temple of the Spirit of God, having been raised up with Christ, a house of spiritual sacrifices made without hands (2 Corinthians 5:1; 1 Peter 2:5). Has there ever been a temple that can do anything on its own or serve a purpose other than host its sacred objects and people of worship? Indeed, the Tabernacle of God's holy presence dwells within us.

We are individual parts that make up the fullness of Christ's body (Ephesians 1:23; 4). Can a hand, foot, eye, mouth, ear, or any other body part function without the Mind, which is Jesus (1 Corinthians 2:16)? Every part must be connected to the Head, to Life Himself.

We are sheep, often found wandering (Ezekiel 34:31; 1 Peter 5:4). Are sheep mighty or independent? As lambs, can we protect ourselves from imminent danger, let alone take care of our daily needs without the good Shepherd? Trust that the lack of intelligence and strength in these animals was no mistake when Jesus compared us to them.

We are children, having been adopted by our Abba as sons and daughters (Galatians 4:6; Ephesians 1:5). What child upon this Earth has survived, let alone been born, without at least one parent? Wonderfully, we have a Father who calls us His own and loves us extravagantly, despite our frequent prodigal-like wastefulness and waywardness.

Finally, we are a bride (John 3:29; Revelation 19:7). We may reach this picture and finally interject, "Aha! Yes, a bride can do something on her own." True, a *woman* can do something on her own, but can a bride? What is the purpose of a bride but to be one with her groom, receiving his family name and entering his home?

Similarly, we should remember that, just as Eve was taken from the side of Adam and fashioned into a woman, we too were taken from the side of Christ upon Calvary so that we might be fashioned into His future wife (Genesis 2:21-23; John 19:34). We would have no breath or any good thing without our glorious Groom and His preparation of us (Revelation 21:2). Hear Him serenade us even now, "You are bone of My bones and flesh of My flesh" (Genesis 2:21-23).

In the growing absence of stained glass cathedral windows, let us paint these pictures upon the interior walls of our hearts, allowing the light of God's Word to shine into us so that we may view them ever more clearly and brightly (Psalm 119:105). We are branches that can do nothing apart from Him. We are temples that can do nothing apart from Him. We are rocks that can do nothing apart from Him. We are body parts that can do nothing apart from Him. We are sheep that can do nothing apart from Him. We are children that can do nothing apart from Him. Corporately and conclusively, we are a bride who can do nothing apart from Him.

As incapable as these images may make us feel, God does not want us to despair. The full picture is that we are apart from Jesus no longer. There is something glorious ahead for each of us in the radiant image of Christ.

THERE IS NO LADDER

I must have a penchant for pain. Though acknowledging my inability without Jesus has grown easier over time by His grace, I remain stubborn. His love utterly disarms me even during my most impressive fits of argumentative foolishness, yet still, it seems I return regularly to the wrestling ring with my Lord (Genesis 32:22-32). Outmatched, God puts His finger on my hip and effortlessly presses, "What is your *true* motivation to do nothing?"

I hear the pop. I crumble to the ground. I whimper.

While I would relish portraying myself positively, revealing an admirable man of respectable spiritual stature, I cannot lie to anyone, let alone myself. My motivation to do nothing can often be found rooted—yet again—in my desire to do something. As much as I could fervently, even sincerely justify these intentions as those in which I seek to please the Lord, they are often nothing more than if-then statements of my own creation. "*If* I do nothing for long and hard enough, *then* the Lord will prepare me to do something great for Him and His kingdom," I argue in the back of my subconscious. Sometimes these thoughts even make their way to the forefront of my consciousness, all hidden motives aside.

Perhaps others have found themselves tracking along similar trains of thought. Who are we fooling, though? Is the Lord not nearer than our own thoughts (Matthew 9:4)? Can He not disclose our innermost secrets (1 Corinthians 14:25)? If it is any comfort, it is as though we walk in the twelve disciples' dusty, worn sandals. As Luke recounts, "An argument arose among them as to which of them was the greatest. But Jesus, knowing the reasoning of their hearts, took a child and put him by His side and said to them, 'Whoever receives this child in My name receives Me, and whoever receives Me receives Him who sent Me. For he who is least among you all is the one who is great'" (Luke 9:46-48).

As much as we may trick ourselves into thinking that we would never argue about our greatness or so unabashedly seek God's acclaim, Jesus knows what transpires in the shadows of our souls. We often categorize doing nothing as a checkbox on our spiritual task list that must be crossed off before moving onto doing something significant. We cannot view it like this. In fact, no significant work will ever be assigned to us if we continue thinking this way. This is as wrong as scheming, "If the last shall be first, I better line up to be last because then I'll make it to first place one day." God knows our hearts and, oh Lord, He knows mine.

Even if we do not immediately feel the same, certain questions require sincere consideration. What do we believe we can do on our own? What do we actively do in our lives and ministries? And most importantly, why do we do those things? Allow the Spirit to penetrate between soul and spirit, revealing the true reasons to us; it is no use hiding from the living Word (Hebrews 4:12-13).

Nothing is not the first rung to climb before the next rung, up the spiritual ladder. There are no rungs. In fact, there is no ladder. Even the ladder that Jacob saw in his dream at Bethel was not revealed so that we might climb up to heaven or serve as our pathway into His throne room (Genesis 28:10-17). It was a shadow foretelling of God's incarnation in Jesus. He came down to be with us so that we never need to climb anywhere (John 3:13; Ephesians 4:19-20). We have already risen and remain seated with Christ in the heavenly realms right now, no ladder required (Ephesians 2:6; Colossians 3:1; Hebrews 4:16).

More difficult questions will eventually confront us all. What if God never helped us accomplish the dreams we have for ourselves, or perhaps, even for Him? As well intentioned as our hopes may be, what if they are not the ones Christ intends for us? Are we willing to give up our expectations of kingdom service and greatness entirely?

Perhaps the plans God has made to prosper us look like nothing more than that which David declared as a young shepherd. "Be still, and know that I am God" (Jeremiah 29:11; Psalm 46:10). As I grow in Christ, I am increasingly convinced that the Lord has a far less busy life in store for me than I am naturally inclined toward.

Of course, I am not saying—nor do I expect—that God intends for us to sit in a perpetual state of quiet stillness over the remainder of our lives, never doing anything whatsoever. Both scripturally and experientially, we should agree that there is far more to the normal Christian life than this. However, we should also recognize that modern Christians have missed how much quiet, peaceful, and inactive nothingness the Lord does intend for His people (Genesis 25:27; Ecclesiastes 4:6; Isaiah 30:15; 32:18; 2 Thessalonians 3:12; 1 Timothy 2:1-4).

We have largely forsaken His will for our own, especially when our will sounds "good." Just because something is good does not mean it is *His* good for us. We would benefit by eliminating this kind of misleading thinking from our minds. I will be the first to admit such elimination is necessary for me.

To be clear, I am not here to tell even one person what doing nothing looks like specifically in their own life. That is the Holy Spirit's job. But before we can take another step forward in what He does have for us—before we should do anything else, before we even *can* do anything else—Jesus waits for us to fall on our knees, surrendering even our most well-intentioned "kingdom-building" and "God-glorifying" plans to Him.

God sent His Son down so that we never need to use one bit of our own strength climbing upward. He is God with us and there is nothing we have done, can do, or ever will do apart from Him. Behold the mighty and incomprehensible grace of our ascended King Jesus, through Whom we have been saved from sin and death, in Whom we now sit at the right hand of God His Father, by Whom we live filled with His Holy Spirit (Acts 13:52; Romans 5:10; Colossians 3:1). He is Everything. Should we desire to level up in accomplishing absolutely anything, we can do nothing apart from Jesus.

QUESTION

What can I do?

ANSWER

Nothing.

READ

John 15

REFLECT

- What self-made achievements and titles do you lean on for your worth? If those disappeared, where would you find your worth?

- Do you believe the responsibility to work lies with you, or with Jesus? What "responsibilities" are most difficult to relinquish?

- What have you believed you can do without Jesus? After reading these last few chapters, how might that be changing?

- What is your favorite picture of the church that is used in scripture? What else can you learn and apply from that image to your life?

- What has been your secret motivation to living out Christ's words? Do you have any aspirations in God's kingdom that need to die?

HOW DO I DO NOTHING?

Let us therefore strive to enter that rest...
Hebrews 4:11

THE STRIVING IS REAL

As mind-numbingly elementary as doing nothing sounds, there are few jobs more difficult. We are quite oriented to doing something, and with good reason. This is the message being taught to most Christians today. Churches everywhere have begun to sound little different than activist groups and political committees, even intertwining these types of causes with the bride of Christ. American Christians have predominantly placed their stock in both the well-meaning left of social welfare and justice as well as the fundamental right of national freedom and liberty, picking their respective sides as though these are the battles God cares about most. "If you love Jesus, you must do something," we are regularly pressured into believing. But our battle is not to be fought against flesh and blood (Ephesians 6:12).

One could easily argue that many people within the church remain too complacent, and this activism message is what's needed today. But it isn't. While the message to do something resonates deeply with sincere believers hoping to make a difference in the world, it is missing the main point of Jesus and the much bigger vision He has in mind. Sadly, this popular message of the age has led many Christians to lead lives of fleshly whims and powerless self-dependence. I raise my own hand in admission.

As a result, our most important work does not begin in asking what we should do next. Our portion of work begins in resisting the natural desire to do anything whatsoever by our own strength. This will sound familiar, surely, for in this basic theology is where we find one of the foremost differentiators between Christianity and other religions. Though most religious traditions instruct their adherents to do the "right" things and follow certain rules, practices, and traditions, Christianity preaches a rather opposite position.

We should remember Martin Luther and the church Reformation came against this false gospel of legalism and its widespread teaching back in the early sixteenth century. Our passionate brother brought into fresh light the good news that "By grace you have been saved through faith. And this is not your own doing; it is the gift of God" (Ephesians 2:8). Framed in even simpler terms, we can say that we have been saved because God did something, not because we did anything. Praise Jesus.

Grievously, the gospel of legalism is still alive and cancerously circulating within the body of Christ. Too many of our fellow brothers and sisters have been led astray from the gospel of grace to which we were all won. While refuting this gospel may seem like an unnecessary task so long after the Reformation, it is important to realize that the weed-like, strangling tentacles of legalism have still wrapped their way around the pulpits that preach amazing grace, however sweet the sound.

It does not end here, either. There are some within the church who have unfortunately accepted a gospel that Dietrich Bonhoeffer labeled "cheap grace." These fellow saints have been misled into thinking that we can do anything desired—even nothing if that's preferred—because of God's free and undeserved gift of salvation. While doing nothing may be acceptable among such Christians, it is certainly not the commonly taught best practice.

Lastly, legalism is often found thriving within our own hearts and minds. Even if we use different language, we hold ourselves to a standard of performance and unattainable merit that has been placed upon us by no one other than ourselves. We too often forget—or altogether miss— the new life in the Spirit we have received, where there is "now no condemnation for those who are in Christ Jesus" (Romans 8:1).

In every branch, denomination, sect, and leaning of Christianity, we will find the message persists, disguised in all sorts of seemingly harmless, theological, and do-gooder vernacular. Once the mask is off, though, it's unmistakably dangerous and ugly. *Work. Earn it. Try harder. Make it happen.* Yes, the popular message whispered, shouted, and prayed among Christians begins to sound eerily close to familiar advertising slogans: *just do it.*

Translated from a series of messages that became the book, *The Life That Wins*, radical Chinese missionary Watchman Nee urged believers, "They know God's way of victory. But they do not have the faith. They know their inability. But they do not know Christ's ability. They see the total corruption of their flesh. But they do not see the riches of Christ as God's gift to them. How do we receive this gift? By doing nothing. Let us simply accept it. As we believe God's word, we receive His gift. This is the gospel."

Accepting this true gospel, what does the Bible more accurately have to teach about how to do nothing apart from Christ? Hebrews offers a unique insight into our part of the work equation. Here we find a reminder of the grace which we have received in abundance. "For whoever has entered God's rest has also rested from his works as God did from His" (Hebrews 4:10). While that alone sounds stupendous in its past tense phrasing, we cannot conclude with these words. This state of rest does not manifest itself as easily as we may at first expect at first. Scripture continues, "Let us therefore strive to enter that rest, so that no one may fall by the same sort of disobedience" (Hebrews 4:11).

Striving and *resting* are not words we often find so explicitly linked together. They do not complement one another like milk and cookies or peanut butter and jelly. At first glance, this odd couple sounds as incompatible as oil and water. How can work, striving, or effort possibly have anything to do with resting? Human wisdom would be right to see that a great divide exists between these ideas.

As a recovering doer, I will be the first to admit that my tendency is for action. I want to do as much as humanly possible, saying "Yes" to every opportunity presented. "No" is not a word that I find easily accessible in my vocabulary. As a result, rest is one of the most difficult acts I can possibly take. Quite literally, I find resting to require strenuous intent and effort.

I know there are many others like me, too, precious men and women of God who are on a mission to do something—anything—for Jesus. Or for the world. Or certainly, sometimes just for themselves. Not everyone has these *do, do, do* tendencies, I understand, but there is no denying it: we are legion.

So, the inner conflict arises. As easy as doing nothing may sound to some of the Christian population, for a great many of us—most of us, I would argue—it sounds nearly impossible. Living in this day of hustle and bustle, the disease of doing more has been mistaken for some form of nobility. Resting may seem a bit easier than doing absolutely nothing, but even rest feels impossible when addressed directly. And to be honest, that's part of God's strategy, inviting us into a deeper faith. We have been granted the Spirit of Christ to make this impossible work possible (Matthew 19:26).

Doing nothing does not begin by laying in our bed looking at the ceiling until we audibly hear the voice of God directing us to go somewhere and do something. Not at all. Doing nothing begins merely by "making every effort" to make zero effort of our own. This is hard, difficult work, it turns out. More importantly, it is an act of obedience, as the book of Hebrews confirms. Or, as Watchman Nee plainly observed, "This is the gospel."

Maybe this is the reason that "resting" sounds so much like "wrestling" at first listen. We must each wrestle against the culture, even culture within the church, to rest. And yes, we must also wrestle within ourselves to do the same. Yet God invites us all into it. Rest is not as easy as it first sounds. It is hard. Or as many say today, the struggle is real.

Now we have something worth striving toward.

HANDCRAFTED DELIVERY

"I t is finished" (John 19:30). Christ's final words at Calvary are, debatably, the most important words ever spoken about the future of humankind and God's kingdom in this present age. Triumphantly, Jesus declared in His dying breaths that everything He had come to do had been completed exactly as purposed by God (Ephesians 1; 3:11). The veil of the temple ripped in two, the dead walked among the living, and the Earth literally shook after they were spoken (Matthew 27:50-53).

As a nearby centurion aptly responded to these events, "Truly this was the Son of God" (Matthew 27:51-54)!

Unfortunately, it seems that we quite forget these conquering words as His followers, commonly living as though there remains a great deal left unfinished. In no uncertain terms, we fail to take our King at His word or understand the magnitude of work that His cross victoriously accomplished on our behalf.

Years ago, my life felt like it was flipped upside down. While praying for a word about the new year and what Jesus would have me focus on, I very abruptly heard, "Get a job." Having been a full-time entrepreneur working for myself over the previous six years, I did not at all expect this. But I had come far enough over my history with the Lord to know that I would be wise to respond quickly. So, I emailed some other business owners I knew and, by the grace of God, was hired that next week into what many would rightly consider a dream opportunity.

Rather quickly it became obvious that the timing could not have been better, as God's instructive guidance was an immediate precursor to what became the worst month of my life to date. Jesus faithfully provided a new and stable position while everything else shook around me—my family's health failed, household expenses mounted, deep friendships faltered, business ventures suffered ruin. It felt like a hurricane had come to sweep up everything in its path. Fortunately, like a storm, the worst of it was over quickly and the rest of that year became one of the best of my life, quieter and more peaceful than any I encountered before it. It truly was a calm after the storm.

Fast forward one year. As other doers will sympathize, given my personality, it didn't take long before I started to feel antsy again. With twelve months of rest under my belt, coming to consider it much like a sabbatical year, I began to fast and pray near the end of that season about what the following year would hold. I thought to myself, "I've rested long enough. Now it's time to figure out what's next." *What's next* are my code words for trying to get ahead of myself—and the Lord. Still, I fasted, waiting for my Counselor to speak.

Three days before the end of my fast, I had a vivid dream. In it, I heard a knock at my front door. Answering, I greeted three delivery men with a bed. Only, this was no normal bed. It was twice as tall as my home's ceiling and wider than the perimeter of my otherwise large master bedroom. Additionally, the bedframe was wood, engraved ornately with gold in its carved areas. This looked like it belonged in the bedroom of a king.

Surprised, I said, "This isn't mine. It's not my style." Still dreaming, I could clearly see the bed which I had ordered instead, explaining to the delivery men that it was a chic gray, just big enough to fit me, and very modern looking. It appeared nothing like this comfortable, yet royal monstrosity in front of me.

One of the delivery men studied an order form on his clipboard. "No, this is yours. It's already been paid for. And frankly, we wouldn't even know what to do with it if you didn't take it." His heavy breathing implied it had taken quite a bit of maneuvering to arrive at my doorstep.

Without another option, I shrugged my shoulders and accepted the gargantuan delivery. "I guess I'll take it," I said, a little put out by the whole ordeal. To my chagrin, the bed was mine.

God's hilarious. I woke up before dawn, instantly chuckling at His sense of humor. Not a moment later I felt the Lord impress upon my spirit, "The amount of rest that I have for you is so much more extravagant than you have space for in your life. But it is at your doorstep. I've paid for it. Why would you turn away what I've made and delivered to you?"

Jesus, Carpenter that He is, handcrafted and sent His rest to me. In fact, He's handmade that rest for every one of us who will believe and obey, striving to enter it. Sometimes His rest shows up on our doorstep, and we just have to accept it, whatever ordeal it may be to fit into our lives. Other times, we may have to wait a little longer, or even lay aside the burdens and weights impeding such rest—which we will consider how to do together soon (Hebrews 12:1). Whatever it is we can do to enter His rest, it is imperative we do it.

These ideas may seem incompatible at first, I admit it. Are we to do something, or aren't we? A little bit of both. To be clear, the thing that we must do to experience His rest is believe that the work He set out to accomplish truly is finished, and everything that He paid for has become readily available to us. In other words, receive that which He has already done for us, purchased with His very life. That still sounds like doing nothing to me. Just welcome His grace, ineffable and infinite. We can only obtain what He has paid for, not attain it ourselves.

Put another way, our effort lies not in doing something and saying, "We did it." It looks like us coming to the foot of His mighty cross, soaked by His precious blood, proclaiming in awe and praise, "Jesus did it." To rest in doing nothing apart from Christ, believe everything of greatest importance has already been completed, once for all. Yes, everything.

On a personal note, I very much wish that the church continued to refer to following Jesus in the same manner that the first-century church did. They did not speak of themselves only as a religion. In fact, the word "Christian" is used a sparse three times in the New Testament, which means "follower of the Anointed" in Greek (Acts 11:26; 26:28; 1 Peter 4:6). In the book of Acts alone we find the church referring to themselves as belonging to "the Way" more than all references to "Christians" throughout the New Testament (John 14:6; Acts 9:2; 19:9, 23). Even Paul introduces himself as "a follower of the Way" to Governor Felix (Acts 24:14, 22).

Our forerunners in the faith knew that they had found the Entrance to a whole new kingdom that knows nothing of the works-based effort typical in other religions. Of course, this was not an easy thing to accept, especially for Jewish people who had lived according to the Law for thousands of years. This is one reason we have entire books in the New Testament dedicated to refuting legalism. But overall, these converts were disciples of Jesus who declared and invited others with confidence to join them in the Way. This invitation remains open today.

The Bible alludes to entrances regularly—gates, doors, paths (Matthew 7:13-14; John 10:9; 14:6; Revelation 3:20). In this, we will discover the truth that Jesus is our one and only Way to rest, for He is Rest incarnate (John 11:28-29). If we do not see Him for who He truly is and what He has fully done, looking instead for what we can do, we will altogether miss the rest He has for us. We will shut the door on what Christ has used His nail-pierced hands to sand, construct, and carve for us from the lumber of His marvelous cross. Listen, He stands and knocks (Revelation 3:20).

Lord Jesus, be our Way. Be our Rest.

ONWARD UNPARALYZED

To understand what rest may look like in our own lives, it will help to also understand what rest is decidedly not. This is imperative if we wish to accomplish anything with Jesus.

There are entire movements within the church teaching people that God has a perfect will in every little thing we do—when we wake up, what color shirt we wear, which direction we take at a fork in the road, and so on. Though this may seem extreme, I have met many Christians deeply afraid of frustrating or even sinning against the Lord with their action or inaction, their speaking or silence, their left or right. How terribly exhausting.

The well-meaning but misguided belief of those who practice this lifestyle is that consulting the Lord for every decision is their attempt to be filled with His Spirit, abide in the Lord, and depend on Him for everything. While I definitively agree the church at large can use more practice in fervently seeking after the Lord's regular counsel and occasionally foolish-looking wisdom, this line of thinking does not lead unto resting in Him (1 Corinthians 1:20). Instead, this kind of thinking leads to Christian paralysis, where believers become lame and stunted in their ability to follow Jesus over the long haul, often unable to discern even basic wisdom for themselves.

Consider the maturing of children. While young, they are completely dependent on their parents. When my three children were toddlers, for example, my wife and I needed to provide them instruction with step-by-step details: how to put on their clothes, how to eat at the table, how to make their bed, and so on. But as they matured, our instruction lessened to: please get dressed, please eat breakfast before we leave, please make sure your rooms are clean. Over time, our guidance grew largely irrelevant, as they became tasks that all my children learned they needed to complete regardless of their parents' direction.

Is this not also true of us as we mature in the Lord? Should our Father have to order our every single step? Indeed, in Him, we have life and move and breathe, unable to do anything apart from Him. But Christ is not a life respirator, He is our Life. Relying upon the Lord's instruction for every movement we make is not a life of maturity, but immaturity. God only encourages that we maturely acknowledge every movement we make is impossible without Him, nothing more.

The Bible has several examples in which the most faithful of God's servants didn't wait for the Lord's instruction. They just did what they thought was best in the moment (Acts 15:22, 25, 36-41; Philippians 2:25; 1 Thessalonians 3:1). In Proverbs alone, we can find a treasure trove of such instruction, with example after example of wisdom being that which we should seek. Solomon writes bluntly, "The beginning of wisdom is this: Get wisdom, and whatever you get, get insight" (Proverbs 4:7).

With Christ alone as our Wisdom, we should all seek the wisdom to be found in Him and given by Him. This may regularly look like what the world would label wise. Or it may look foolish (1 Corinthians 1:30; Colossians 2:1-3; James 1:5). Whatever the case, it is wisdom that makes our way forward possible (Proverbs 4:10-13). Under the wide and protective umbrella of God's will, there is far more latitude than we might suspect. Move in the liberty of Jesus.

Years ago, I was serving as the CEO of a user experience design and software development agency. Through a few rapidly unfolding events, it became clear to me that I needed to move on from that company to something else. But I had a hang-up: I had no clue what I would do in its place. So I went to the Lord in prayer, asking for His direction. "Lord, all I want is what You want. What do You want me to do?"

The response I discerned felt sudden, unexpected, and welcome. "No, Jonathan, what do *you* want to do? Write it down." Surprised, but excited, I quickly took to pen and paper at a coffee shop and wrote down what my ideal days, weeks, and months would specifically look like in my work moving forward. Without exaggeration, not thirty seconds after I finished my list, I received a phone call from an old colleague that allowed me to cross off the first two items on my list. As the new year rolled around that next month, I established more specific goals to achieve by the coming March. God accomplished those for me just one week into January. I stood by, effortlessly watching the Lord work, amazed and grateful.

I cannot say that this is prescriptive for every person or every situation. There have been plenty of times in my own life that the Lord carefully instructs me which way to go, even contrary to my own desires. But the more I walk with Jesus, the more my will has aligned with His. When my three children come to me now about what they should each do, I just as often ask them in response, "What do you think is best?" I need not dictate to them, just as our Lord so rarely dictates to us. He invites, He draws, He encourages, and He admonishes, but with rare exception does He force our hand at anything. This is walking in the way of His rest, carrying the light burden of His easy yoke (Matthew 11:30).

While resting in the Lord may very well require we stop, or at least pause certain activities, it should not look like paralysis. Then again, our resting in the Lord may also have us begin other activities which we would have no inclination—or should have no business—starting on our own. Life in Christ is composed of seasons and rhythms, ebbs and flows, hills and valleys, much and little. We will consider the seasons of life soon enough. The main point to consider at this moment is what our resting should look like in daily experience.

To fully discover rest in the Lord, do we need to stop something? Or perhaps, is the Spirit encouraging us to start something? Or even more likely, are we supposed to simply take a few moments to be still and know that He is God before we keep stepping forward in what it is we already know needs accomplishing today (Psalm 46:10)? Whatever the case, we should not fear that we may take one misstep if we move forward at all. This is not the will of God for anyone in Christ Jesus.

He is always calling us forward, whether His way forward for us looks like an intense pace, a casual walk, or even a standstill to the rest of this world. Onward we move in Him.

ENTERING THE FIRE

Vacations. Hammocks. Massages. Sleep. Television. Weekends. Several thoughts may come to mind as we consider rest, each person with their own preference. But are these ideas what God had in mind when He rested on the seventh day of creation (Genesis 2:2-3)?

We return to Hebrews, which already reminded us that our obedience requires resisting our effort to work. We will now choose to rest in the perfect work of Jesus, just as God did in Genesis (Hebrews 4:10-11).

While this scripture about rest may be one we have heard regularly on its own, it is rarely taught in partnership with the passage that immediately follows it. Continuing, we read, "For the Word of God is living and active, sharper than any two-edged sword, piercing to the division of soul and of spirit, of joints and of marrow, and discerning the thoughts and intentions of the heart. And no creature is hidden from His sight, but all are naked and exposed to the eyes of Him to whom we must give account" (Hebrews 4:12-13).

In addition to the dichotomy we found between rest and striving right before it, we are now introduced to the concept of rest and the Word of God being in concert with one another. But what in the world does God's Word have to do with rest?

First, it is important we define what Hebrews means here when it references the Word of God. Due to how many Christians have used this term as one synonymous with the Bible, many of us may casually interchange these phrases when we read scripture. Therefore, we might think that the author of Hebrews means to write, "For the [Holy Bible] is living and active…" We would be mistaken though. While scripture indeed contains the *many* words of God, it is not *the* Word of God. Jesus is the one and only Word of God that is constantly being spoken (John 1:1-18). In nearly every instance, it is "scripture" that is referred to when speaking of the written, inspired words of God.

For those of us raised in the church, we have probably even heard Sunday school teachers encourage children to do their "sword drills," making a game of whipping out Bibles to find the correct scripture as quickly as possible. But even the sword is not a book, it is a Person. Paul instructs that we are to each wield "the sword of the *Spirit*, which is the Word of God" (Ephesians 6:17).

This is exactly why the writer of Hebrews can conclude that the Word of God is living, active, sharp, and piercing. While the words that Jesus has spoken through scripture can still become alive to us today by the power of His active Spirit, a book can never come alive on its own. This is why this passage concludes, "And no creature is hidden from *His* sight, but all are naked and exposed to the eyes of *Him* to whom we must give account" (Hebrews 4:13). Let us reconsider our vocabulary so that the only Word which scripture and Spirit ever speak about might remain continually and articulately proclaimed: Jesus.

With this understanding, to further discover the correlation between rest and the Word of God, we will turn to whom the writer of Hebrews often refers as a shadow of Christ—Moses. After God's covenant is confirmed with His people in the desert, the Lord invites Moses up Mount Sinai to wait for His commandments. The Old Testament describes, "Then Moses went up on the mountain, and the cloud covered the mountain. The glory of the Lord dwelt on Mount Sinai, and the cloud covered it six days. And on the seventh day He called to Moses out of the midst of the cloud. Now the appearance of the glory of the Lord was like a devouring fire on the top of the mountain in the sight of the people of Israel. Moses entered the cloud and went up on the mountain. And Moses was on the mountain forty days and forty nights" (Exodus 24:15-18).

God's servant followed the voice of the Lord. But even as he obeyed, Moses was not immediately invited up to the mountaintop. No, he had to wait. "Come up to Me … and wait there," God instructed the prophet (Exodus 24:12). Patient, Moses did not move until God called him into the devouring fire of His glory. It is no coincidence that He drew Moses forward on the seventh day, the day of rest (Genesis 2:2-3; Exodus 12:16; 16:26, 30; 20:11; 31:15, 17, 21; Numbers 28:25; Deuteronomy 16:8; Hebrews 4:4).

Too often, we become impatient waiting for the Word, Jesus, to speak. We would rather avoid the inconvenience of waiting long enough to hear a single thing that the Lord says to us, let alone everything that He wishes to voice beyond this moment. Worse, we often act much more like the Israelites who collectively feared God's voice and elected Moses to relay God's words to them rather than receive it themselves (Exodus 20:18-21).

The first thing we can learn from this story is that receiving the spoken words of Jesus will very often arrive as we respond to the Lord's invitation, "Come up to Me and wait there." God is not mute, He just asks for us to wait. His Word is well worth waiting for. Eventually, as we wait, He will invite us forward.

True, sometimes it takes longer than we wish to enter the rest that He has for us in certain areas of our lives. While we have gained perpetual rest for our souls because of Christ's sacrifice, absolutely, we may not be experiencing the manifested peace of God in all our circumstances. It is in times of unrest, especially, that we will gain much by waiting for the Word (John 1:1-14).

The second thing we can learn from this story is what His rest looks like. Rest is often defined by our own proclivities and cultural norms, leading some to think of beach vacations even as others consider exercises like yoga or biking. While we may again retreat to the ideas that the people in our surroundings commonly equate with rest and relaxation, God's rest appears more like a devouring fire than it does pillows and pajamas or weekends and holidays. Moses knew He could enter the devouring fire of God's glory because He had already seen that God's flame did not consume the burning bush through which he received his first calling (Exodus 3:2). Furthermore, Moses knew he could trust the Lord and that he didn't need to be afraid of the Voice he came to know face to Face (Exodus 33:11).

This is precisely what God's rest has to do with His Word. As we obey in entering the rest that God has for us, it is in our waiting and rest that we will encounter the Word of God which comes to actively pierce us, dividing between that which may otherwise seem as indistinguishable as our soul and spirit. The sword of the Spirit is sharper than we can imagine and will set us on fire for what the Lord will have us eventually do (Ephesians 6:17). But until we encounter a living experience of Jesus Christ, the active Word, we will not proceed forward as effectively as the Lord desires. As Hebrews reminds us, we are all fully exposed to the Lord's sight. Why would we try to outrun or ignore the voice of God in the first place? His eyes are always upon us.

Responding to His Word is required to more fully enter His rest. It's His Spirit that bears fruit. It's His Spirit that gives life. It's His Spirit that expresses God's love. It's His Spirit that empowers us. And this is just a taste.

Fortunately, the author of Hebrews does not end there, either. In gracious conclusion, we are reminded that "we do not have a High Priest who is unable to sympathize with our weaknesses…. Let us then with confidence draw near to the throne of grace, that we may receive mercy and find grace to help in time of need" (Hebrews 4:15-16).

Rest requires we draw near to—and even enter—the burning, devouring fire. It is there, in His gracious, sympathizing presence that the Word will refine us, but not consume us (Zechariah 13:9; Malachi 3:2; 1 Corinthians 3:12-15; Hebrews 12:25-29). He has come to help us in our time of need. May we wait for and encounter the piercing, living Word of Jesus Christ. His burning glory awaits us as we do.

ABANDON ALL FRUIT BASKETS

In nearly any professional environment, people measure some aspect of their organization's performance. Profit, sales, conversions, growth rates, customer satisfaction, responses, and an endless stream of other metrics are constantly being monitored and reported. This helps further explain why we may be so inclined to doing something, as the somethings we often carry out give us yet one more measurement by which we can track what we deem as success.

I'm at fault too, having maintained my own personal dashboard to keep me focused and on track. *Am I accomplishing what I "need" to accomplish? Have I hit my made-up milestones? Have I achieved my fabricated goals?*

Unfortunately, even our churches have turned to similar metrics. Rather than focus on the quality of life that the Lord is producing in our communities of faith, we have frequently resorted to attendees per week, programs per month, and dollars per year. The problem with this is not entirely in the act of measuring our progress alone, but in the metrics we choose to track. Put plainly, the goals we establish and numbers we measure rarely have anything to do with the growth that Jesus desires in us. The results that God prevailingly seeks first involves our inner growth, then emerges in our outer growth.

The apostle Paul recognized this profoundly. The church planter writes, "Are we beginning to commend ourselves again? Or do we need, as some do, letters of recommendation to you, or from you? *You yourselves* are our letter of recommendation, written on our hearts, to be known and read by all. And you show that *you* are a letter from Christ delivered by us, written not with ink but with the Spirit of the living God, not on tablets of stone but on tablets of *human hearts*. Such is the confidence that we have through Christ toward God. Not that we are sufficient in ourselves to claim anything as coming from us, but our sufficiency is from God, who has made us sufficient to be ministers of a new covenant, not of the letter but of the *Spirit*. For the letter kills, but the Spirit gives life" (2 Corinthians 3:1-6). In short, we should be caring about lives changed over bodies present, depth over breadth, and quality over quantity.

As we study Paul's example further, we find that he did not even evaluate himself. To Corinth, he explains, "But to me it is a very small thing that I may be examined by you, or by any human court; in fact, I do not even examine myself. For I am conscious of nothing against myself, yet I am not by this acquitted; but the one who examines me is the Lord" (1 Corinthians 4:3-4, NASB).

It is common to desire some form of measurement, of course. Measurements can help us identify the outward signs of our inner growth, encouraging us onward in the Way. So how is it that we can know our lives have been replaced by Christ's life, our hearts openly testify of Jesus, and we are growing in Him? Because fruit is being produced (Matthew 7:17-18; 13:23; Mark 4:20; John 15:2, 8, 16; Romans 7:4).

Our expectation and desire to bear spiritual fruit is not wrong in and of itself. We should desire—and even expect—to bear it, because Jesus said we will do so as we abide in Him. The life-giving seed of His Spirit has been placed within us so that His fruit will grow (1 Corinthians 15:45; Galatians 5:22-25). The problem with our effort to track our growth, however, lies once again in our focus.

We become so fixated on our fruit-bearing that we forget Who it is that grows this fruit in the first place. It is not our striving to produce love that reveals love. It is not our desire to manifest joy that exudes joy. It is not our squashing fear that grants peace. Branches do not put on a fancy suit and power tie so they can go to God's Kingdom, Inc. and meet management's quota.

The fruit we bear is the fruit of God's Spirit, produced by the Life of Jesus Christ that He has granted to everyone who believes in Him. Period. In our pursuit of the fruit rather than the Source of all fruit, I believe we may even be unintentionally quenching the role of God's Spirit (1 Thessalonians 5:19). I know I have. To bear fruit, we solely need to seek the Life.

Even as I have increasingly learned what it means to abide in the Vine so that He might channel His Life into my otherwise lifeless branch, I must share my verifiable weakness in the matter. Many years into my marriage, my wife and I were praying in bed when she received a very direct exhortation for me. Nicole humbly offered, "The Lord has a deeper place of trust for you, and as you venture there, you will experience greater intimacy with Him." Immediately, I started racking my brain to take inventory of where I might not be trusting Jesus. My family, my work, my finances, my very life—I couldn't think of anywhere prominently apparent where I lacked trust. But the Spirit confirmed the word within me. I knew Nicole was right.

Over the next month, I prayed devoutly about where the Lord desired greater trust from me. I agonized over it, desiring nothing more than to accept His invitation and experience greater intimacy with Him. Finally, after much reflection and prayer, the Lord pointedly and mercifully revealed, "You don't trust Me with other people. Am I not their Father, too?" He was so gentle, but I was undeniably shaken.

In my self-justified pursuit of the God's will, I have too often tried to "help" other people, doing everything I can to turn, push, pull, yank, force, and get them to where they "should" be, according to my own calculations. This is especially true of those closest to me. Ultimately, I have assessed others' fruit-bearing abilities. From the vantage point of my own branch, I have secretly (and not-so-secretly at times) tallied the depth of the fruit baskets being filled by other branches to measure them against my own. I sought to taste others' fruit, disgustedly spitting out much of it when it has not met my pharisaical standards. In other words, I have horrifically judged the specks in my brothers' and sisters' eyes while logs remain in my own (Matthew 7:3-5).

In Bob Goff's book, *Love Does*, every chapter opens with a single, straightforward sentence about how he changed during his walk with Jesus. I will never forget one lesson he shares, specifically. I can still see the words on the page, as crystal clear as when I first read them: "I used to want to fix people, but now I just want to be with them." Oh my.

I am still learning what it means to trust Jesus with others—and it's not like I have trusting Him with myself down to a science, either. I need to trust God more with my wife. With my kids. With my church community. With my friends. But by God's sheer grace, I am fully convinced that we should abandon our petty fruit baskets and learn to restfully abide in Christ as He uniquely leads us. He deals with everyone differently than He deals with me because, as it turns out, He knows them far better than I do. Imagine that.

Any measure of faith and fruit that our lives may manifest have been authored and assigned by Him in the first place (Romans 12:3, Hebrews 12:1-2). Any lack that we may experience at a certain point in our walk is not meant to be measured against and looked down upon, but so that the Spirit and body of Christ might fill that lack according to His provision in our times of need (1 Thessalonians 3:9-13; James 2:14-17). We all have need. I know I certainly do.

Practically speaking, life is just better this way. Asking for God's goals rather than our own, gauging our spiritual health less, and wholly devoting ourselves to the only One who can accomplish what's necessary is a whole bunch easier. It happens to even grow bunches of whole, beautiful, ripe, delicious spiritual fruit. I can't tell you how much more this approach grows exactly, as I lost my fruit basket a little while back. I just know it tastes better.

QUESTION

How do I do nothing?

ANSWER

Rest.

READ

Hebrews 4

REFLECT

- Where is resting hard work for you? Where do you still feel or place a burden upon yourself to strive out of your own strength?
- Where do you not have space for rest in your life? What would it look like to accept the rest that Jesus has handcrafted for you?
- Are you afraid of taking a misstep in God's will? How has reading this alleviated some of that unnecessary pressure?
- Are you taking the time to wait for God's living Word? What has He actively revealed when you have taken the necessary time?
- How will you focus more on pursuing Life than growing fruit? Where has fruit been produced in your walk without any effort?

WHAT ON EARTH IS JESUS DOING?

*So Jesus said to them, "Truly, truly,
I say to you, the Son can do nothing
of His own accord, but only
what He sees the Father doing."*
John 5:19

THE RIGHT QUESTION

I n 1896, an American minister by the name of Charles M. Sheldon published the book, *In His Steps*. While this title may sound unfamiliar to many Christians today, its subtitle probably won't: *What Would Jesus Do?* Nearly a century later, this became the motto by which many Protestants and Catholics lived their lives, sporting the trendy bracelets with its popular—and regularly parodied—acronym, WWJD?

Though the motivation of this campaign and its literary inspiration was no doubt well placed, there is a reason it is so recent. It has nominal biblical support. This is not the Way that we were actually taught to live by Jesus and the early church. We have not received the indwelling life of Christ so that we can go about our days and decisions trying to figure out what Jesus *might* do in a given circumstance, marching forward with our fingers crossed, hoping we make the right choice. Quite the contrary. We have been given His Life so that we might live by it (Galatians 2:20). Our life is long gone (Romans 6:4; 2 Corinthians 4:10-12).

In other words, we have been asking the wrong question. Rather than try to resolve something with our own limited understanding, contextually trying to apply first century ideas to twenty-first century living, we have been given the very same Spirit that Jesus operated by daily (Romans 8:11). We no longer must live our lives trying to determine what is good or evil—or as we more often might weigh, good and best. Living like this is no different than everyone on Earth has lived since Adam's fall. Saved or unsaved, anyone can know what's "good" and try to do that very thing. We now eat from the Tree of Life, not the tree of knowledge (Genesis 3; Proverbs 11:30; 13:12).

The Father looks upon us from heaven and says, "These are my sons and daughters, with whom I am well pleased" (Matthew 3:17; Mark 1:11; Luke 3:22). Adopted, we have each received the exact same gift of Fatherly pleasure that Jesus received, His anointing inside us (1 Corinthians 2:12; 1 John 2:27). He is available to us without limit (Luke 11:13; John 3:34). Even Jesus said it was better if He left so that He could send the Helper to us, ensuring we never have to try and figure out what He might possibly do any longer (John 14:16-17, 26; 16:7).

So, if WWJD is the wrong question, what should we be asking instead? As in everything, Jesus lived out the answer. Meekly, Christ declares, "Truly, truly, I say to you, the Son can do nothing of His own accord, but only what He sees the Father doing. For whatever the Father does, that the Son does likewise. For the Father loves the Son and shows Him all that He Himself is doing" (John 5:19-20). If we did not understand Him the first time, our Lord emphatically continues, "I can do nothing on My own. As I hear, I judge, and My judgment is just, because I seek not My own will but the will of Him who sent Me" (John 5:39).

This changes everything. Or at least, it should. Jesus did not go about His ministry asking, "What would Abba do?" He lived in a daily, ceaseless communion with His Father, freely answering the more important question, "What is Abba doing?" Ignore the fact that this new question only changes a few small words. If we each lived in a similar way, the shift would be titanic. Once applied, our lives will never be the same.

First, this new question prompts us to acknowledge who really does the work. Since all authority has been given over to Christ by the Father, it would be beneficial for us to ask not what Jesus *would* do so we can do that on our own (Matthew 28:18; Ephesians 1:20-22). Instead, we should ask what Christ *is* doing so that we can partner with Him in the effort. Our doing should simply follow His doing.

Second, this question transitions everything into the present tense. Rather than consider Jesus a mere historical figure who would have had the right answer in a given situation, we can approach Him as the all-knowing, uncontainable, living God of past, present, and future who has been, is currently, and will be doing something in every moment and corner of the world. We can only do something right now because He is doing something right now.

These two points were reinforced for me with my daughter, Riley. One morning I was putting away dishes in the kitchen. It was a very basic task that I had no challenge finishing on my own. As I worked, my eldest sauntered past me. Captivated with joy just by looking at her, I asked, "Hey Riley, do you wanna do the dishes with your dad?"

Passing by, my ten-year-old smiled sweetly at me and answered, "No thanks."

Depending on everyone's childhood or parenting experience, some may expect the story to turn in an unpleasant direction at this point. But, please understand that I remained sincerely unoffended by my daughter's response. There was not one ounce of me that grew disappointed or angry, bemoaning, "Why would you not want to work with me?" Instead, I very calmly responded, "Okay, I love you," before continuing ahead with my work.

"I love you," she agreed, walking to the other room. Even though she had not accepted my invitation to work with me, I resolutely knew the love in her heart for me. Even in her declination, I could hear that she didn't wish to hurt or neglect me, she just wanted to do something else at that exact moment. So, she ventured off to begin what she had in mind as I continued forward with the task I was committed to finishing.

As soon as our exchange ended, I perceived Jesus illustrating to me, "This is My invitation to you always. I am completing the work with or without you. But I want you to join Me so that We might do it together." What a God we serve.

For myself as much as anyone, it is time we begin asking the right question. Even though we may not choose to participate, sauntering past our Father who tirelessly labors on His children's behalf, God is already at work. He has not left us to finish the job without Him. Wondrously, we have been invited into His labor (Matthew 9:38; Luke 10:2; Ephesians 2:10). More often than we realize, Jesus seeks to work *in* us, not just through us. Even still, in every work, He continually invites us to collaborate with Him as He remains faithful to accomplish it (Philippians 1:6). For He cannot deny Himself (Philippians 1:6; 2 Timothy 2:13).

In our severely misplaced belief in what we can do, we have fallen into the unfortunate though prevalent trap that the Jews also fell into as they went about performing their religious duties. After His own declaration that He could accomplish nothing but what He saw His Father doing, Jesus warns, "You search the Scriptures because you think that in them you have eternal life; and it is they that bear witness about Me, yet you refuse to come to Me that you may have life" (John 5:39).

Framed in more modern vernacular, we ask what Jesus would do because we think that our efforts and ambitions hold the secret to a well-lived life. But the key to successful living lies not in our misplaced questions, logical deductions, or faulty judgment calls. It rests in simply loving and following Him.

All that to ask: *What is Jesus doing?* Or if we prefer keeping with culture's trend toward brevity, WIJD?

EXERCISING DISCERNMENT

"**A**mazing Grace, how sweet the sound; that saved a wretch like me; I once was lost, but now am found; t'was blind but now I see." We may know the lyrics, but how many of us truly feel as though we can see that much more clearly? Perhaps some light has made it through our previously darkened eyes, but does our new sight in Christ amount to as much help as we hope for in our daily experience?

Jesus had quite a bit to say about our senses. For example, He quotes Isaiah, "For this people's heart has grown dull, and with their ears they can barely hear, and their eyes they have closed, lest they should see with their eyes and hear with their ears and understand with their heart and turn, and I would heal them" (Matthew 13:15). He is the amazing Grace to which our eyes have each been opened, assuredly. But unfortunately, despite the Light that has opened our eyes, we have not trained our spiritual senses, so to speak. We poorly see what He is doing on the Earth today (John 8:12; 1 Timothy 6:6).

This is why we do not find Jesus actually posing the question throughout the gospels, "What is Abba doing?" He just watched Him. The Son was in close enough proximity to His Father, eyes in wide open focus upon Abba's handiwork, that Jesus could faithfully partner with God in that work. Again, it was Christ who professed, "the Son can do nothing of His own accord, but only what He *sees* the Father doing" (John 5:19).

See, one of our chief problems lies not solely in the unspiritual question we have gone about asking ourselves, "WWJD?" The staggering epidemic in the church today is that she does not have her eyes open to the movement of God. Our spiritual sight remains like that of the blind man at Bethsaida who began to see some blurred, unclear shapes, but not everything (Mark 8:22-26).

We must let Jesus restore our sight entirely, going to Him so that our spiritual eyes might be opened to the work that He is accomplishing everywhere we look. Instead, we stagger around with cloudy vision at best, or worse, our eyes locked shut. We would be wise to heed the pronouncement of Jesus, "If you were blind, you would have no guilt; but now that you say, 'We see,' your guilt remains" (John 9:41). We need God's anointing salve for our eyes (Revelation 3:18).

It's not our sight alone that lacks, either. The Lord was just as clear about our hearing. Over and again, Jesus exhorts anyone in earshot, "He who has ears to hear, let him hear" (Matthew 11:15; Mark 4:9, 23; Luke 8:8; 14:35).

Paul warns Timothy, too, "For the time is coming when people will not endure sound teaching, but having itching ears they will accumulate for themselves teachers to suit their own passions, and will turn away from listening to the truth and wander off into myths" (2 Timothy 4:3-4).

Have we not similarly turned aside to the voices that better suit our desires, be that the enemy's, the world's, our family's, or even our own? True, we may not think that we close our ears to scripture, but when the living Word of Christ's Spirit comes to correct, exhort, nudge, or lead us in a direction, do we listen? Too many of us have taken the controller and pushed the mute button on Jesus.

Even at that, there is still much of God's written word that we ignore, as well. When we feel our conscience quicken in response to scripture, we so often justify our inaction by convincing ourselves that God means those words for others. The challenging truth must be faced: if we will not allow both His written and spoken Word to work within us, how can we ever expect Him to work through us? In *The Pursuit of God*, A.W. Tozer aptly declares, "The Voice of God is a friendly Voice. No one need fear to listen to it unless he has already made up his mind to resist it."

Now, if our spiritual senses and instincts require equipping for God's work, how is it that we might prepare them?

We do not need holy glasses and heavenly hearing aids, we need spiritual discernment. This was Paul's prayer for the church in Philippi, just as much as it should remain our continued intercession for the church today. "It is my prayer that your love may abound more and more, with knowledge and all discernment, so that you may approve what is excellent, and so be pure and blameless for the day of Christ" (Philippians 1:9-11). Here we learn that discernment is the act of approving God's always excellent work. This cannot be done through natural means alone, either; it requires the Holy Spirit (1 Corinthians 2:6-16).

In this very generation, discrimination has been something that many have fought against in the workplace. Rightfully so, for mistreating people because of their race, gender, age, sexual orientation, or beliefs should have no part of our new life in Christ. Let us testify to the good news that *all* people have been made in His image, regardless of their sin, brokenness, or differences from us.

However, there is one particular discrimination God does desire from us. Spiritual discernment necessitates we learn to vehemently discriminate against any work that has not been originated by God in His workspaces. Discernment in the Spirit affords us the ability to separate between that which is initiated by ourselves and that which is initiated by Jesus. As the psalmist reminds us, "Unless the Lord builds the house, those who build it labor in vain" (Psalm 127:1).

Unfortunately, saying we need discernment—or even asking God for more of it—does not automatically grant us more discernment. Hebrews reveals, "But solid food is for the mature, for those who have their powers of discernment trained by constant practice to distinguish good from evil" (Hebrews 5:14). The church lacks practical training in this regard today. Who among us is going about the Christian life, exercising and encouraging the "constant practice" of our discerning powers? Even now, I feel the Lord tugging on my heart to do better at this myself, equipping others in heightening their spiritual discernment.

One Saturday afternoon, I was driving home by myself. Out of nowhere, the thought popped into my head that I needed to visit my old church that evening. Given the fact that I hadn't been there in years, the thought felt rather random. Curious, I quickly tuned into the idea as though I had too hurriedly skipped past a radio station broadcasting a faint signal. As I mulled it over, I realized that I didn't even know what time their service now began. Then another so-called thought just as quickly responded to my inquiry, "5:15." Okay, I was getting the point.

"Anything else?" I asked God. As soon as I posed the question, I saw a faint but identifiable picture in my mind of a very specific location in that church's nearby courtyard, a short distance away from the primary worship building. Knowing it is the Word who spoke everything into creation, His voice also loves to paint images (John 1:1-3; Colossians 1:16).

Once home, I told my wife Nicole that we needed to visit the church by 5:15 in the evening. Packing up our kids, we left our house to arrive at our destination what happened to be fifteen minutes before the service began, as instructed. At that precise moment I heard, in that exact location I faintly saw, an old acquaintance, Jeremy, slowly made his way towards me. He was heading to the parking lot to leave. Happily, I greeted him, caught up with him briefly, grabbed his phone number, and said I would call him.

Though my family and I stayed for worship, my assignment was complete. Had I been there a moment later or entered the church building to meet and greet old friends, I would have missed Jeremy altogether. He only visited the church that one service with another friend, not to return anytime soon.

While I didn't know it at the time, Jeremy planned to leave for China just six months later. During that season of his life, he had no other Christian community to encourage him in his young faith. Though I didn't know Jeremy particularly well before then, I met with him regularly after that Saturday evening until he left to teach children overseas later that year. Had I not focused in on my so-called random thought, I would have missed what God was doing.

My point in sharing this story is that our random thoughts may often be the very specific thoughts of God. Sometimes they are just what we assume—random ideas that we can ignore. But more often than we may expect, Jesus is trying to grant us His mind (1 Corinthians 2:16). God's voice usually sounds no louder or much different than our own thoughts, either, which is to say that He is a gentle Father who prefers not to raise His voice at us. Though we may be waiting for burning bushes accompanied by the booming voice of James Earl Jones in surround sound, as the prophet Elijah encountered, the Lord does not solely speak through mighty signs; He often just whispers (1 Kings 19:11-13).

It doesn't always make sense, of course. Even the apostle Peter was originally confused by the unexpected visions he received about unclean animals, but this picture is how God began to extend His gospel to the Gentiles (Acts 10:9-20). As a general principle, the more unexpected, even unwanted a thought first strikes me, the more it prompts me to pray and discern what God may be trying to reveal through it. This kind of exercise is far more rewarding (and less physically demanding) than going to use weights and do cardio. It's kind of like God's gym.

Years before that spiritual workout, I had a close friend, Kenny. One afternoon the thought dawned on me, "Give Kenny money." As clear and sudden as it was, I knew that this had not been my own idea, so I obeyed quickly. Finding my checkbook, I mentally prepared to give him a few hundred dollars.

But as I reached the amount line, I felt stopped, prompted, "Less." Naturally, I first thought that this may be my own will rather than God's, selfishly trying to hang onto a little more for myself. But as I conversationally asked the Lord about it, I became convinced that He wanted me to give Kenny less money than I had planned upon first hearing the instruction. So, I paused to ask how much to give, waiting until Jesus gave me a very specific amount. And He did.

Handing Kenny the check a few days later, I told him I had no idea what it was for, only that it was intended as a blessing. I didn't go into all the details about my exchange with God about it. Kenny thanked me, and that was that. Or so I expected.

Two weeks later, Kenny called to thank me again. While I couldn't pick up at the time, his voicemail was testimony enough. "Jonathan, thanks for being obedient. My car broke down yesterday and the check you wrote me paid for the repair with just three cents more than I needed." Pausing, he joyfully concluded, "Yeah, God's good."

I concur. God is so very good. Jesus cares to reveal Himself to us and through us in astoundingly personal ways. But we must be open to those ways. Had I not heard or responded to, "Less," sure, Kenny would have still had enough to pay for his repair. But God wanted to show this brother—and me—how specific His provision is. Our Provider isn't looking to just meet our needs reactively. He is also proactive, knowing what we need even before we do.

The Lord is constantly speaking to us and shining His light upon the path in front of us, one step at a time (Psalm 119:105). We can discipline our senses and practice discernment so that we might become even more useful vessels for Him and His work. Do not quench the revelation and testimony of Jesus Christ through whatever supernatural means He decides to use (1 Thessalonians 5:19-21; Revelation 19:10). If we cannot feel, see, or hear Him clearly, we will be workers without the strength to fulfill every work He wishes to accomplish through us as His servants.

I have no monopoly on sensing God work, so please know these types of stories await every one of His children. There are so many true tales like these from other saints that they could fill libraries. If someone's personal experience is limited in this arena, there are other books I highly recommend that delve more deeply into how believers might each discern the voice and work of God. *Jesus Speaks* by Frank Viola and Leonard Sweet is one such title, offering abundant biblical examples and fresh insights. Reading practical books like this should be part of every Christian's exercise regimen.

Just remember, pastors, authors, even the early apostles have been given no special, upgraded version of the Holy Spirit. There is no spiritual seniority or tenure of faith required to experience Him in these ways. We each have the same, communicative God abiding, moving, acting, emoting, and speaking within us. However, while there is no rank and hierarchy in the workplace of God, just as in the professional world, we cannot expect to fulfill the work if we do not have the training—or interest—to execute. Jesus will personally coach us all, but we must decidedly welcome His Spirit's training (1 John 2:27).

After Christ's dire proclamation of Isaiah to the Jews, He goes on to commend His disciples, "But blessed are your eyes, for they see, and your ears, for they hear" (Matthew 13:16). Our eyes have all been opened to the Light of Jesus, and our ears have all been opened to the Way. As His sheep, we already know His voice (John 10:4). But we should not end here. There remains more. There is always more with Jesus.

Practice makes perfect. This saying exists for a reason and remains just as true of spiritual discernment. Perhaps we should edit the adage only slightly: practicing discernment makes perfected disciples. Let's start hitting God's gym more regularly. He wants to strengthen us for His work.

COMMUNITY REQUIRED

Nobody likes going to the gym alone. Okay, perhaps that's mainly me speaking. But the statistics do show that individuals who share a workout buddy remain more likely to continue their healthy habits. In fact, one study proved that merely hanging out with healthier people more often will lead those who struggle with obesity to lose more weight over time compared to those who spend time with those like them.

Just as most physical exercise is more difficult—and less fun—when on our own, exercising our discernment is no different. We are wired for community. God does not want us wandering alone, braving things by ourselves. Never. Living the Christian life as God intends it is impossible without His people. Quite simply, community is a non-negotiable in the life that Jesus desires for us.

Though I was raised in the church, I did not fully understand just how essential Christian community—the *ekklesia*—was to my knowing and discerning Jesus until I encountered something of a shakeup in my church experience. After being married to Nicole for a few years, we grew unenthused by the local nondenominational Bible church we were attending. Though I fully know the church is God's people, not a place, "attending" is the appropriate word to use here, because that's all we were doing at the time. We came and we went, sneaking in and out of pews with no one else to notice. Though many other wonderful members appreciated participating in that part of Christ's body, Nicole and I were not experiencing life with them any longer.

After a short while there, by truly strange means—a story for another book, I'm sure—Nicole and I were led to a much smaller church on the other side of town. In it, we encountered people who not only knew God was at work behind the scenes, they expected His Spirit to work front and center. This was not an expectation of demand, as some communities' misappropriated expectations can sometimes become; it was an expectation of faith. Theirs was a belief that Jesus speaks today—everyday, actually—and He would speak to and through His people as we earnestly desired Him to do so (1 Corinthians 12:31; 14:1, 39).

This experience changed my outlook entirely. I could share countless testimonies of hearing, seeing, and watching the Lord work in ways that can exclusively be described as supernatural, but I would digress in doing so. While many may synonymize "supernatural" with "miraculous," let me be clear. Yes, I have witnessed and experienced miracles of God that have forever impacted me. But these are rare, as much as I know they are happening all across the world. Here, I am merely encouraging a life of the supernatural, in which Jesus breaks in and gains the credit as we clearly experience activity that cannot be accomplished in our natural strength. The warning of scripture still stands, "The natural person does not accept the things of the Spirit of God, for they are folly to him, and he is not able to understand them because they are spiritually discerned" (1 Corinthians 2:14).

To practice a life of supernatural God invasion, we need to join an expectant people. There is no other way to partake in all that God is doing. Let us each hope to find and join a tribe who seek to know and discern the Lord's activity in their lives, for it is the Lord's work that will transform us. Nobody else's work alone can do that.

Even if our current church community does not demonstrate expectation exactly like this, there is no need to be discouraged. Even in our respectable, perhaps cautious Christian communities, God remains at work. Nobody needs to use language like, "God told me" this, "the Lord God Almighty says," or "I am seeing God" do that. In fact, using this kind of terminology can often make other believers feel inferior to us. Honestly, language like this is used with rare exception in the New Testament. We do not need to work up the Holy Spirit like a wind-up toy monkey. Though He is supernatural, He is just as often super...natural.

Furthermore, while we should each be training our senses to discern what God is doing in this very moment, even the most faithful and tenured saints who distinctly know the voice of the Lord will admit that they might be wrong at times. No Christian has the edge on discerning correctly, 100% of the time. As much as some eyes may be wide open, we all still see dimly (1 Corinthians 13:12).

This is precisely why scripture teaches that we need God's people in the first place. "For we know in part and we prophesy in part," Paul writes to Corinth (1 Corinthians 13:9). As a result, we are instructed to practice discernment with the entire community of Christ. The apostle encourages a replicable method to create such a safe space for practice: every time the saints gather together. "For you can all prophesy one by one, so that all may learn and all be encouraged, and the spirits of prophets are subject to prophets. For God is not a God of confusion but of peace" (1 Corinthians 14:31-33).

How very practical the epistles remain to this day. I like to call this the musketeer model, offering a one-for-all, all-for-one opportunity to practice discernment. Everyone should have the opportunity to engage in this sort of spiritual exercise and encouragement. As we become informed about how God's Spirit organically works, desire Him to work, and practice that work, we will all be amazed by what He does (1 Corinthians 12:1, 31; 14:1, 26-33).

The Bible has much more to teach us about our need for others, as well. Two are better than one (Ecclesiastes 4:9). Two will withstand an enemy (Ecclesiastes 4:12). Where two or more are gathered, there is Christ (Matthew 18:20). Of course, Jesus could have chosen to live out His incarnation self-sufficiently, as an enigmatic figure to the world until His death. But the Creator of our universe sought to live out His ministry on Earth with twelve other men—not to forget the company of His many beloved sisters, either. Though we may not always be aware of it, Jesus continues walking out His interdependent, shared life with us to this day (1 Corinthians 12:12).

My family and I have since moved on from the church that God brought us to for a very intentional season of four years. While there, we were effectively equipped with fellow saints to exercise discernment in understanding visions and dreams; sharing and receiving words of knowledge and words of wisdom; distinguishing between spirits; speaking in and corporately interpreting tongues; and sharing and judging prophecies, which always testify of Jesus (Daniel 1:17; Romans 12:6; 1 Corinthians 12; 14:1-33; 2 Peter 1:21; Revelation 19:10).

Only, I prefer to use simpler, less mystical language now. As succinctly as possible, I believe the Spirit continues acting today through painting pictures, speaking words, thinking thoughts, feeling emotions, and, in all of these, pointing to Jesus. The key to engaging His presence is in discerning His movement, and that is best accomplished where He continues living His life today—with us, His disciples.

Since then, Nicole and I have continued our faith journeys with other precious saints after we followed the Lord to help plant an organic Christian community meeting in Phoenix. I could share story after story about how I have received specific discernment and direction from Jesus through the members of this community, as well as other Christian communities among which I am blessed to take part.

But of course, the Christian life is not solely about us and what we need individually. I do not gain greater discernment in my life so that I can horde more words from God in these communities. Sadly, it seems many believers are out to seek the Lord's voice primarily for themselves. I have been guilty of this, too. The problem is, He isn't always communicating to us or about us. Jesus has lots to say, but even more so, He has lots of people to speak to. As a result, God doesn't want us in the ekklesia so that we might solely hear and see Christ more for our own benefit, but so that we might hear and see Him more for others.

This is the corporate work of God. He does not ask us to labor with Him so that we might be personally served in doing so, even as we may seek to hear, see, and discern His activity for this very reason at times. Rather than seek self-help, we should follow our humble King's example, who demonstrates, "I did not come to be served, but to serve" (Matthew 20:28; Mark 10:45).

Before I joined an expectant community, I did not hear Jesus nearly as regularly or as articulately as I now do. The Lord has moved in my brothers and sisters to affect me profoundly. Participating in the church is a requirement for discernment to be experienced more frequently, and God's intention for every one of us is that we discover such a people (Hebrews 10:25). While there are lonely wilderness seasons for many of us along the journey, let us all pray—and diligently seek—to find a tribe who is willing to lay down their lives for one another, build each other up, and mutually seek to ask what Jesus is doing on the Earth.

God is always at work, He just happens to work overtime from home. There's no place like home, and we are the home He is building. His ekklesia. His disciples. His people. His family.

CHANGING SEASONS

"For everything there is a season, and a time for every matter under heaven: a time to be born, and a time to die; a time to plant, and a time to pluck up what is planted; a time to kill, and a time to heal; a time to break down, and a time to build up; a time to weep, and a time to laugh; a time to mourn, and a time to dance; a time to cast away stones, and a time to gather stones together; a time to embrace, and a time to refrain from embracing; a time to seek, and a time to lose; a time to keep, and a time to cast away; a time to tear, and a time to sew; a time to keep silence, and a time to speak; a time to love, and a time to hate; a time for war, and a time for peace" (Ecclesiastes 3:1-8).

Solomon's wisdom and poetry about the seasons of this life are unmatched. But scripture doesn't end with Solomon's thoughts on the topic (Daniel 2:21; Act 1:7;

1 Thessalonians 5:1). Spending enough time in Christian circles, we are bound to hear or even reference our seasons at some point. But what is meant by this idea, exactly? What will we each gain from living our lives according to the season?

First, we have all been around the block long enough to agree that the seasons of our lives do not arrive in expected patterns, as spring, summer, fall, or winter do. Life's seasons come at us more like rhythmic waves than they do predictable periods of time, almost impossible to plan for and often challenging to understand during the encounter. Without advanced warning, some seasons might overcome us just as a tidal wave of freezing, powerful ocean water can. Then again, with even momentary notice of their impending arrival, we may enjoy them with childlike glee. Without identifying the seasons correctly, anticipating their coming or their going, we may very well feel like we are drifting, even drowning at times.

Perhaps the Lord will have us beginning something in one season. In others, He may have us stopping something. Then again, maybe He will have us maintaining much in another season. I once heard the successful CEO of a Fortune 500 company give similar advice. Every three months, this incredibly busy leader took time to evaluate what he was doing, asking himself three basic questions: *What activity am I doing that I need to stop? What activity am I doing that I need to continue? What activity am I not doing that I need to start?*

How incredibly practical. These questions don't need to be reserved for billionaires like him, either. We can ask these same questions of the Lord. It is helpful to determine what Jesus would have us start, continue, and stop. Discerning the seasons we are entering, encountering, or exiting can help us adjust our spiritual eyesight to see what He is doing right now. In other words, to discern the present, sometimes we require the larger context of what has led up to and will follow this very moment.

I have gone about this practice in various ways for myself. When the new year approaches, for example, I carve out focused time after Christmas to seek the Lord in prayer. During it, I ask Jesus for a single word to distill the coming season, waiting however long I must to hear Him. Sometimes I receive words that I might very much expect and gravitate towards naturally—verbs of action and direction. However, there are many years in which I have received foresight from God that I do not anticipate (or particularly want) to hear—words like *with, flourish*, and *perfected*. Upon hearing them, I then look for scripture to help reinforce their themes. Using the words just mentioned as examples, Genesis 5:24, Psalm 92:13, and 2 Corinthians 12:9 uniquely ministered to me during those seasons.

Having done this for fifteen years, it is the lessons of these more surprising seasons that I recall most. By taking barely any time out of my schedule so that I can reflect on the season past and discern the season forthcoming, I have been granted encouraging insight from my King as years ebb and flow into one another. Certainly, I do not always understand the full meaning of each word as soon as I take hold of them, but they consistently help frame what I may encounter in the months that follow.

In a more frequent discipline, I have enlisted the practice of setting my sights on one goal every quarter. Maintaining singular priorities has helped me plod forward in my walk with the Lord, surrendering over more of myself and marking my life with consistent, even if slow, progress. As one of the richest people in the world, Bill Gates, has been quoted, "Most people overestimate what they can do in one year and underestimate what they can do in ten years." Slow and steady is what's needed, and this is no less true—perhaps even more so—in our walk with the Lord. He is at work in us, always inviting us to participate in His meticulously prepared purposes.

Let me be clear though. Over the many years doing this, I have learned my lesson in thinking I can understand the season I am entering purely based on the seasons I have encountered historically. Jesus is regularly doing something new (Isaiah 42:9; 43:19; Hebrews 8:13; 9:15; Revelation 21:5). I am the first to admit my proclivity for frameworks and methods and checklists, but these rarely work in the economy of God. I cannot apply the wisdom of this world to my growth, for God's ways look quite counter to what the world calls progress at all. In the kingdom, wisdom begins with foolishness (1 Corinthians 1:20-27). Greatness begins with the least (Luke 9:46-48). Power begins with weakness (1 Corinthian 12:9; 2 Corinthians 13:3-4). Life begins with death (Romans 5:10; 6:4).

Again, there are seasons for everything. Some are rewarding. Some are challenging. Others are absolutely terrifying. But in each of them, God is at work. Agreed, His work may not be as visible or interpretable as we hope, but we can trust that He is making all things new (Revelation 21:5). This is not hyperbole, it is a reality. All things are being made new by, in, and unto Christ Jesus.

Critically, let us distinguish this practice of discerning the season from trying to figure out what's next. We don't need to be anxious about tomorrow or try to plan our own steps (Proverbs 16:9). Worry is totally unproductive and unhelpful (Matthew 6:27). His steps are the only ones we need to look for today. Jesus desires for us to walk in the Way He has already established for us (Ephesians 2:10). The footsteps have been laid out, and the end of our stories have been written in Christ. He does not need trailblazers, He wants trail-treaders.

Again, I confess my own weakness in too regularly trying to figure out what's next so that I might write my own story and determine my own steps forward. There is a subtle, but dangerous line between trying to discern what Jesus is doing so that we can *partner* with Him, versus trying to figure out what He is doing so that we can *control* our way forward. When any of us deal with these thoughts, we can turn to the birds and flowers as our examples (Matthew 6:25-34).

In her book, *Everything*, Mary DeMuth offers wise insights into this kind of behavior. She writes, "Control is the inner disease of those who need stability and order to function. It is the shiny little idol we worship without noticing." Ouch. I feel that one.

"You shall have no other gods before Me," declares the Lord (Exodus 20:3). Still, we regularly look away from Jesus, replacing our trust in Him and His seasons for clarity we can control. We try to force God's seasons into a calendar we can understand rather than discern and enjoy them for their unpredictable, baptizing impact as waves.

One of my dear friends, Mark, regularly testifies about how God told him to surrender clarity long ago. He had once made clarity his shiny little idol that DeMuth similarly made of control. Personally, I prefer the word choice of "clarity" over "control" because most Christian circles regularly teach our need to solely trust that God is in control. "Nope, not me. I've given God control," I lie to myself. Yet, here clarity stares me in the face, control's more presentable cousin, no less detestable at its core.

As Job declares, "'Who is this that hides counsel without knowledge?' Therefore I have uttered what I did not understand, things too wonderful for me, which I did not know" (Job 42:3). If God is clear on what He intends to do, that should be clarity enough for me. I must frequently repent, remembering that God is very clear on His purposes, even if they remain shrouded in mystery to me.

In the end, we should give up trying to figure everything out. We so often enter hypothetical planning mode, looking to gain foresight into what's coming around the bend to pad and safeguard our own comfort levels. On the other hand, discerning every season is a practice of rest and wisdom. It is a humble position in which we can go before our Lord to ask, "What are you doing in this season, Jesus?" Then, we should quickly conclude, "I give You control of it."

Maybe there's a name for the season we are entering. Or a verse. Or a word. Or a song. Or an impression. Or even instruction. Life is beautifully composed of much and little, highs and lows, starting and stopping, waiting and working, noise and silence, understanding and mystery. But in every season, rest beckons us as we trust in God's good and faithful intentions for us (Jeremiah 29:11). As He gives us discernment through life, Jesus gains more territory in our hearts, and we gain victory over our false, monstrous yet miniscule idols.

Say goodbye to calendars, clarity, and control. Just dive in to enjoy the waves of every season with Jesus. It's quite refreshing.

SPIRITUAL AMBITIONS

Ambition is not something most people consider very spiritual. And with good reason. When we think of ambition, we often correlate it with the fleshly pursuit of worldly power, greed, and success. As much as a lopsided prosperity gospel has infiltrated too much of the church, these fleshly aims have absolutely nothing to do with the full gospel of the kingdom.

I can reflect on my life similarly, quite disappointed by the ambitions I maintained early in my professional career. My drive was wasted on activities that accomplished little with Jesus. In fact, when inspected with spiritual eyes, they are activities that amounted to nothing whatsoever. The modern-day equivalent word that Paul uttered to compare all he had forsaken for the surpassing knowledge of Jesus Christ would be appropriate to use in my case were it not a four-letter word that conservative Christians might stumble over (Philippians 3:8).

Despite my failures, the Lord has been merciful, simultaneously enlightening me to my failures and turning my worst "rubbish" into material He can use for His purposes (Romans 8:28). As author Frank Viola has correctly observed and communicated, "Jesus writes straight with crooked lines." Praise God that nothing is wasted in the economy of His kingdom. Jesus loves to recycle what appears unusable into something quite usable.

To further distance us from such pursuits, the Bible has some rather negative things to communicate about ambition. Paul told the Philippians to condemn teachers who proclaim Christ out of selfish ambition, exhorting the church to do nothing in service of self or conceit (Philippians 1:17; 2:3). James similarly warned against jealousy and selfish ambition, calling it the breeding ground for every vile thing (James 3:14-16). Their words were strong, to say the least.

Interestingly, in the four biblical instances that we find every negative mention of ambition, they are always correlated with selfishness, plainly calling it "selfish ambition." As it turns out, this distinctive adjective is used because there exists a positive counterpart to the self-serving sin.

I have a friend named Austin. He is a brother in Christ who asked to meet with me regularly as he walked out his new marriage, growing career, and burgeoning faith. In speaking temperately of his professional ambitions one afternoon, a question came to mind. "Those are fine goals," I commented. "But more importantly, what are your spiritual ambitions?"

I had never considered this concept before, having largely given up the possibility of ambition being a good thing. We often will avoid the terminology altogether given how much selfish ambition exists in the world. But there is indeed an ambition to be found in Christ.

Notice, Paul writes to the Romans, "I make it my ambition to preach the gospel, not where Christ has already been named, lest I build on someone else's foundation, but as it is written, 'Those who have never been told of Him will see, and those who have never heard will understand'" (Romans 15:20-21). To the church in Corinth, the bondservant openly professes, "Therefore we also have as our ambition, whether at home or absent, to be pleasing to Him" (2 Corinthians 5:9, NASB).

These sound like very different ambitions than those we often encounter within society. Where selfish ambition focuses entirely on serving ourselves, spiritual ambitions rest on preaching and pleasing Jesus Christ wherever the opportunity exists. We may not regularly approach God's kingdom opportunistically, as such a perspective has also been twisted by the world. Yet spiritual ambitions are even more opportunistic in nature than those of the world, for these pursuits store up treasure in heaven (Romans 10:12; Ephesians 3:8; Colossians 2:2). It is work never done in vain (1 Corinthians 15:10, 58).

After my conversation with Austin, I sought to personally explore this concept further. At my desk one morning, I asked Jesus how to discern between ambitions that are selfish (pleasing solely to me) from ambitions that are spiritual (pleasing wholly unto God).

The first impression I received was that Christ-honoring ambition is always initiated by His Spirit, not by myself. Makes sense. I can reflect on the work of my hands and point very quickly to what has been instigated by God versus what has been instigated by me. In the poetic words of T.S. Eliot, the things I start on my own typically end "not with a bang but a whimper." Our own starting should always begin where the Holy Spirit begins, nowhere else. Otherwise, our efforts will end in needless frustration and disappointment (Psalm 127:1). Believe me, I'm a pro.

In his seminal book, *The Normal Christian Life*, Watchman Nee puts it like this: "Origin determines destination and what was 'of the flesh' originally will never be made spiritual by any amount of 'improvement.' That which is born of the flesh is flesh, and it will never be otherwise. So anything for which we are sufficient in ourselves is 'nothing' in God's estimate, and we have to accept His estimate and write it down as nothing. 'The flesh profiteth nothing.' It is only what comes from above that will abide." Nee continues, "We cannot see this simply by being told it. God must teach us what is meant, by putting His finger on something which He sees and saying, 'This is natural; this has its source in the old creation and did not originate with

Me. This cannot abide.' Until He does so, we may agree in principle, but we can never really see it … But there will come a day when God opens our eyes."

Even as a serial entrepreneur and starter, my ability to start cannot outdo His. As my faithful brother predicted, I didn't learn this truth just by reading it. Once again, our innermost eyes must be opened to see what is started by Christ versus what is started by us.

The second thing revealed to me was that spiritual ambitions always produce lasting fruit. Paul instructs the church in Corinth to help build God's house carefully (1 Corinthians 3). We will consider more of what Paul means by this passage later, but what is important to review now is his reason for this caution. He writes, "each one's work will become manifest, for the Day will disclose it, because it will be revealed by fire, and the fire will test what sort of work each one has done. If the work that anyone has built on the foundation survives, he will receive a reward. If anyone's work is burned up, he will suffer loss, though he himself will be saved, but only as through fire" (1 Corinthians 3:13-15).

We should not focus primarily here on the reward Paul mentions. Instead, we can ask ourselves what work of ours will survive until the end, passing through the consuming fire of God's judgment (Deuteronomy 4:24; Isaiah 33:14; Hebrews 12:29). This does not need to intimidate us or cause us to fear, but it can help provide us with a filter. Will the work we do stand everlasting, extending long after our fleeting lives?

Guaranteed, the work we do on our own will not last. Human work is highly flammable. There is just one house that will stand forever, passing through the testing fire, and that house is His church of living stones, the people of God. This does not mean we need to quit everything and become missionaries in a third world country—there is more than enough that the Lord would have us do wherever we currently find ourselves. But it does mean we need to recalibrate our ambitions to become those that God has for us rather than our own. Anything else will amount to ash.

Though these first two insights were welcome, they did not greatly surprise me. There is scripture after scripture to reinforce these points. But then, the last insight came. It nearly knocked the wind out of me.

More than an impression, I heard the subtle yet mighty voice of God whisper inside me, "Spiritual ambitions will expand your view of Me, not contract it." Examples flooded my mind about where I had unknowingly failed in this regard, tears filling my eyes.

Inasmuch as we often seek to please Jesus in our doing something, even our most well-intentioned ambitions often result in restricting the ways of God to the borders of our own comfort zones.

For example, if the Lord speaks to us through unexpected means, but we have wrongly constrained Jesus to remain vocal today solely in scripture, we will not experience Him working as mightily through His Spirit. Likewise, if our desire for certainty leads us to rigidly gripping onto theologies that do not grant Him permission to remain mysterious—even confounding at times—we confine Him to the boundaries of what we consider safe. As C.S. Lewis writes metaphorically about Jesus in *The Lion, The Witch and the Wardrobe*, "Who said anything about safe? 'Course he isn't safe. But he's good. He's the King, I tell you."

Yes, we often place Jesus in our convenient us-sized boxes, rather than letting Him roam unfettered and free in our minds. Naively, we confine God to our own limits rather than letting His limitlessness push us to new heights and depths. Indeed, Jesus Christ is boundless, and our own borders must expand with Him.

As a result, we need not pack away or eliminate our ambitions any longer. We can just point our ambitions to where the entirety of our life should be pointed—Jesus, the Risen One. As we invite His Spirit to lead us, experience the fruit that He is bearing, and let Him loose in our minds and lives, something will be accomplished. He is doing it, to the glory of His name. Now that is some ambition we can get behind.

QUESTION
What on Earth is Jesus doing?

ANSWER
Discern.

READ
John 5:19-47

REFLECT

- How will asking what Jesus is doing (WIJD) instead of asking what He would do (WWJD) change your perspective and life?

- When is a time you have noticed what God is doing or saying? Where do you want more practice in exercising discernment?

- How have your Christian relationships helped you discern what God is doing in you? Where have you played that role for others?

- Do you try to figure out God is doing so you can trust Him, or so you can control things? What kind of season are you are in now?

- What ambitions currently take up your thoughts and energy? How will the three attributes of spiritual ambitions change your focus?

HOW DO I WORK
WITH JESUS?

*For we are His workmanship,
created in Christ Jesus for good works, which
God prepared beforehand,
that we should walk in them.*
Ephesians 2:10

POOLSIDE PARTNERSHIP

As we realize our inability without Jesus, strive to enter His rest, and practice discerning what He is doing, there remains another principle God wants His followers to learn. As the Creator who established every law of the universe, Jesus could accomplish His work in whatever way He chooses. But for reasons that will remain largely incomprehensible, in His infinite wisdom, He has chosen one primary method through which He will accomplish that work: with us.

That's right. By His very nature, Jesus cannot work alone. Since the beginning, God has been a singular "Us" (Genesis 1:26). According to the plans and will of our triune God, we have been called to and enlisted in His purposes (Romans 8:28; 2 Timothy 1:8-9). Furthermore, we have each been empowered by Power Himself for that work (John 16:7; 1 Corinthians 12:11).

Just as professional ambitions require partnership with others to accomplish work bigger than ourselves, spiritual ambitions will not have us sitting back while God accomplishes the work alone. Neither will the Lord simply dictate to us what He would have us do on His behalf. As Paul writes to Thessalonica, "we sent Timothy, our brother and *God's coworker* in the gospel of Christ, to establish and exhort you in your faith" (1 Thessalonians 3:2).

I hear so many believers—and I have failed in this myself—saying that they wish to do something *for* God. But God does not see us as His employees. He wants us to cowork *with* Him, in the family business so to speak. Though we remain His servants, it does not look like servitude in the world. We are not just serving Him, but we are also serving His purposes. This is exactly what He is doing, too. The Father serves God's purposes. Jesus serves God's purposes. The Holy Spirit serves God's purposes. Likewise, our work with Him serves God's purposes. Therefore, all our shared work collectively serves the ultimate and eternal intentions of God.

As incredulous as this may make us feel, it's true. Christ does not want us running off by ourselves to do good things for Him on our own. As children of the promise, He invites us to join His team and collaborate with Him intimately as He moves about accomplishing everything (Acts 2:39; Romans 9:8; Galatians 4:28). It is time we each enter a lifelong, daily partnership with Jesus. We have each been hired for God's work. What a glorious calling. And what an honor it is to serve with Him.

Of course, coworking with Jesus as partners is far easier said than done. We may believe this to be our calling, but how do we live out that calling? Where do we even begin?

Imagine with me, it's summertime, bright, hot. August days in Arizona were not exactly the weather that most long for, but as a kid, I didn't mind it. Scorching summer days meant one main thing—my brother and I could go swimming. Maybe even our friends would join us, complete with water balloon fights, Super Soaker wars, and a refreshing Otter Pop as we dried off. While every pool experience held its own joys and distinctions, there remained one constant in these childhood moments. I can still hear the patient echoes of my mother calling out to me, "Don't run, walk."

For any of us who spent summers around the pool as a child, we were bound to hear this reminder at some point. Maybe we even enjoyed our swimming seasons at community pools, where warning signs heightened the discretion in prominent red letters. *Attention! No running.* Lifeguards are not hired to look out just for those in the pool, but for those near it, too.

We will discover a beautiful reminder in this necessary caution. It seems there are many of us today who feel like we are running in every which direction. In fact, we may often hear this answer when we ask how people are doing. "I've been running like crazy," the saying goes.

In the church, running seems to absorb our focus as well. With biblical reason, of course. At least two authors cite the race set before us as believers in Christ. Paul writes, "Do you not know that in a race all the runners run, but only one receives the prize? So run that you may obtain it" (1 Corinthians 9:24). Near the end of his life, the apostle later acknowledges to Timothy, "I have fought the good fight, I have finished the race, I have kept the faith (2 Timothy 4:7).

The author of Hebrews also makes mention of this spiritual race, exhorting, "let us run with endurance the race that is set before us" (Hebrews 12:1). As we can see from these verses, there is a race to be run, absolutely. The Bible lays this out with undeniable clarity. However, let us acknowledge here again that our error in urging Christians to run lies not in the encouragement itself, but in our emphasis. Once again, we have placed the onus on ourselves.

Onus is an uncommon word these days. It refers to something that is one's duty or responsibility. The *Merriam-Webster Dictionary* offers a more austere definition, describing it as a "burden" or "disagreeable necessity." But we already took care of that responsibility in answering what we can do—nothing. To be accurate, God already took care of that burden on His cross. While we remain quick to place loathsome mandates and religious duty on ourselves, Christ took every last bit of that off us, onto His capable shoulders. In other words, our "onus" has become "off-us" because of Jesus.

The same can be said of our running. While the scriptures just cited plainly illustrate the race in front of us, there are nearly 350 verses that mention walking. Granted, not every one of these passages specifically refers to our walks of faith, but the comparison remains stark nonetheless: three versus 350. Put another way, 116-times more verses mention walking over running.

If we believe that Christ accomplished everything that is necessary for us to partake in salvation, we can also believe what Paul writes to the Ephesians: "For we are his workmanship, created in Christ Jesus for good works, which God prepared beforehand, that we should walk in them" (Ephesians 2:10). Jesus completed the impossible work. We only need to walk in the work that Christ has prepared for us.

There is no pace that He has commanded us to maintain other than strolling forward in Him, even leisurely if necessary. We don't need to work up our energy and keep charging ahead at a breakneck speed. We need Godspeed. While the Lord may have us sprinting at some points in our faith, even those seasons of running will not be required of us in every season. We have not been called to run worthy of our calling, but to walk worthy of it (Ephesians 4:1; Colossians 1:10; 1 Thessalonians 2:12).

I do not like running all that much in the first place, so this appeals to my sensibilities. However, my next-door neighbor comes to mind. Tommy is the most avid runner I have ever known, what athletes commonly call an ultra-marathoner. He has run more miles than most people would consider casually walking over the next decade, even having completed a 100-mile race in less than 24 hours. Still, as much as he enjoys the painstaking process of training and competing, even Tommy wouldn't be able to run every moment of his life. Such a pace is impossible to maintain in anyone's own strength, both physically and spiritually speaking (Isaiah 40:30).

Fortunately, we have not been asked or commanded to keep that pace. Poolside, like a Lifeguard to His excited children, God lovingly reminds us, "Be careful, just walk." He does not want us slipping or falling (Psalm 17:5; 37:31; 38:16; 56:13; 66:8-9; Proverbs 3:21-23). In truth, He often keeps us from doing so, invisibly holding our hands and sustaining our feet as we carelessly race upon slippery paths (2 Samuel 22:37; Psalm 18:36; 73:2, 23; 94:18).

We may proudly and foolishly presume that we won't fall. Peter thought the same thing. With conviction, the fisherman-turned-disciple told Jesus, "Though they all fall away because of You, I will never fall away" (Matthew 26:33). He was wrong. Peter couldn't make it past morning (Matthew 26:74-75). Even if we have offered up similarly haughty confessions to the Lord before falling flat on our faces, our stories won't end there, just like it didn't with Peter. I know I am often like Peter. Thankfully, Jesus is always like Jesus, faithful despite my unfaithfulness and failings. He knows I love Him, still inviting me to work with Him (John 21:15-19).

God's invitation awaits every one of us. While we may be able to run a lap, a marathon, or, like Tommy, an ultra-marathon, our life in Christ is not intended to be one long, strenuous race. It is a way—or rather, the Way (2 Kings 21:22; Psalm 25:8, 12; 32:8; Proverbs 9:6; 23:19; Isaiah 48:17; John 14:6; Acts 18:25; 19:9; 24:22; Hebrews 13:7). It is a path (Psalm 16:11; 17:5; 23:3; 25:4, 10; 27:11; 119:35, 105; Proverbs 2:20; 3:6; 4:11, 14, 18; 4:26; 5:21; 8:20; 12:28; 15:19; Isaiah 26:7-8; Acts 2:28; Hebrews 12:12-13). It is a journey (Exodus 40:38; Judges 18:5-6; Mark 6:7-9). Just as the tribe of Israel, we too sojourn with the Lord over the course of our lives (Genesis 15:13; 17:8; 26:3; 47:9; Deuteronomy 10:19; Psalm 15:1; 39:12; 119:19, 54; 146:9; Ezekiel 47:23; 1 Peter 2:11). In short, we walk.

Jesus has already prepared every step that we need to walk in, having readied the work He intends for us to help accomplish. In fact, if we think walking sounds better than running, we should go one step further and try sitting. In the book *Sit, Walk, Stand*, Watchman Nee thoroughly reviews Paul's letter to Ephesus, correctly highlighting what proceeds any of our spiritual movement.

Nee writes, "Most Christians make the mistake of trying to walk in order to be able to sit, but that is a reversal of the true order. Our natural reason says, *If we do not walk, how can we ever reach the goal? What can we attain without effort? How can we ever get anywhere if we do not move?* But Christianity is a [strange] business! If at the outset we try to do anything, we get nothing; if we seek to attain something, we miss everything. For Christianity begins not with the big DO, but with the big DONE. Thus Ephesians opens with the statement that God *has* 'blessed us with every spiritual blessing in the heavenly places in Christ' (Ephesians 1:3) and we are invited at the very outset to sit down and enjoy what God has done for us; not to set out to try and attain it for ourselves." Personally speaking, if this doesn't get us singing and dancing in the aisles, I don't know what will.

In our gusto and pride, we may often run ahead as fast as we can, repeating to ourselves, "I've got this." But assuredly, we do not. He's got this. As God encourages us to safely and soundly walk forward, we should trust that He cautions us to do so with our very best in mind. "Okay, Dad," we can each respond, slowing down. Father knows best.

In the strength that the Holy Spirit supplies us, our faith may very well begin flying high before it ever falls to running speed. But eventually, we will all decelerate to the steady way forward that God has for each one of us—a walk. Isaiah says as much, promising that "they who wait for the Lord shall renew their strength; they shall mount up with wings like eagles; they shall run and not be weary; they shall walk and not faint" (Isaiah 40:31). Fly, run, then walk. That is the order of the Christian life. Or if we prefer the New Testament, we can trust the order that brother Nee illuminated in Ephesians, too. Sit, walk, stand. Either way, the average pace of our Christian lives shouldn't feel fast, crazy, or unsustainable. Though we may just be some excited kids eager to do something, we can heed this poolside wisdom and stop running so furiously.

If there is any distance to be run, it is a consistent but unhurried victory lap in the race Christ Jesus has already won. On that glorious day in which we are called home, He will usher us up to the podium so that He might place a winner's wreath of honor upon our heads, triumphantly raising us up with Him who holds the enduring title of First Place (1 Corinthians 9:25; Colossians 1:18, NASB).

The apostle Paul was correct when he observed, "Do you not know that in a race all the runners run, but only one receives the prize? So run that you may obtain it" (1 Corinthians 9:24). Indeed, only one receives the prize, and it is Christ who has already received it. We too will obtain it with Him as we press forward in His footsteps, in calm and steady working partnership with Jesus.

GET ON THE SCALE

One cold November, the night after Thanksgiving, my stomach started aching. I had never experienced anything so agonizing. I couldn't stand. I couldn't walk. Only the noises that my family had to endure from me surpassed my pain. As much as I tried to delay it, this warranted a trip to the emergency room. After a long weekend in the hospital and several tests, the diagnosis revealed my symptoms to be caused by a rare but passing inflammation that mimicked the pain of appendicitis. Two weeks later, I felt just fine.

Thankfully, this experience revealed something else more serious. I had not been taking care of myself. My blood pressure was poor. My cholesterol was high. My blood sugar registered at pre-diabetic levels. And frankly, my weight was higher than I had even anticipated, not having stepped on a scale in far too long. It was then that I determined my life's health habits would not return to usual.

Sometimes, we all need to step on the scale. By this, I do not mean simply checking our physical weight—though this too can be a helpful practice. To experience well-rounded health in our walks with Jesus, we would be wise to each assess where we are lugging around unwanted and unnecessary spiritual, emotional, mental, physical, and practical burdens in our life.

The book of Hebrews agrees. In one of the same passages of scripture wherein we are encouraged to run the race—that is, to move forward in the good work that God has prepared for us—we are also exhorted to remove any unnecessary weight. "Therefore, since we are surrounded by so great a cloud of witnesses, let us also lay aside every weight, and sin which clings so closely, and let us run with endurance the race that is set before us, looking to Jesus, the Founder and Perfecter of our faith" (Hebrews 12:1-2).

In other translations, it says that these weights and sins hinder, encumber, entangle, beset, ensnare, and just plain get in the way. The New Living Translation offers my favorite wording, modernizing the language with great clarity, "let us strip off every weight that *slows us down*, especially the sin that so easily *trips us up.*"

As much as I am learning to slow down my life, that does not mean I want to be slowed down or tripped up if I can possibly avoid it. Does anyone of us want to intentionally slow ourselves down or trip ourselves up? While we may say no, our actions indicate otherwise. More accurately, our inaction indicates otherwise.

Firstly, we cannot ignore the sin that this passage calls out. In fact, Hebrews expands upon its exhortation against sin, urging, "In your struggle against sin you have not yet resisted to the point of shedding your blood" (Hebrews 12:4). In this extreme truth, we may be reminded of Christ's command to remove the eyes and hands that cause us to sin (Matthew 5:29-30). I am not encouraging anyone actually remove their physical body parts if they sin with them, nor do I believe Jesus meant that word for word. Every one of us has sinned, often falling into the same sin over and again. God does not expect His church to walk around with dismembered bodies on His behalf, Paul even coming against those who taught people to mutilate themselves in one of his epistles (Romans 3:23; Philippians 3:2).

However, God definitely *does* want us to remove our "flesh" so that we can walk more freely in partnership with Jesus. That means the areas of our soul life and the vices that enable sin to easily trip us up. We have certainly been forgiven of every sin, in advance, forever (Hebrews 10:10). It's done. There is absolutely no need for shame, guilt, or condemnation in Christ any longer (Romans 8:1). But the ongoing effects of sin still distract and prevent us from experiencing the best life that Jesus wants for us now. Having received His amazing grace and forgiveness, He compellingly invites us in love to do everything we can in partnership with His Spirit to "lay aside" the sin that gets in our way.

There is much more that could be said about this topic, but the removal of sin from our lives has already received enough attention from other books and teachings. This focus is commonly legalistic in nature, instructing—or boldfaced guilt-tripping—that we each try to defeat sin by our own strength rather than learn to walk in the triumph that has already been won over sin once and for all. Once again, we are taught to do everything we can to make our lives better rather than rely upon Jesus.

Still, we should each consider where there remains recurring sin that trips us up along the path that God has us walking. Then, we can seek to get rid of it with Him by doing exactly what Hebrews instructs: "look to Jesus, the Founder and Perfecter of our faith" (Hebrews 12:2). As much as sin may continue to trip us up along His path, He already conquered our every wrongdoing, mess-up, and failure on the cross, including those in our future. It is by His victory that we too can experience victory, exchanging our sinful life with His sinless one. Though we will fail on our own, we can move forward in Christ without guilt and without looking back. Similarly, we will not spend any more time here contemplating sin together.

In contrast to the inordinate focus that sin commands within our churches and consciences, there exists far too little talk of the weights we experience in life. In learning to partner with Jesus, we shouldn't just repent and practice righteousness, we should practically eliminate the obstacles that slow us down (1 John 3:7). We need to cut out the fat, so to speak, thereby enabling our faster movement forward.

This is not to say we need to start running more, as we were reminded poolside by our Lifeguard. But to cowork with the Lord, we will reap huge benefits as we make ourselves able to move more readily, more easily, and more briskly in step with Him. God's children all desire freedom, and this is one pragmatic aspect to walking in the liberty Jesus paid for on our behalf (1 Corinthians 7:21; 2 Corinthians 3:17; Galatians 5:1; 1 Peter 2:16; 2 Peter 2:19).

This is not freedom that comes solely from the Spirit of God. This is the freedom that comes as we sensibly choose to unshackle our lives from everything unnecessary—fears, burdens, worries, negative relationships, old patterns, bad habits, and beyond. This stretches very much into our finances, our calendars, and our material possessions, as well. It comes down to where our allegiances and priorities lie, either with the kingdom of God, or with the world. In this regard, Jesus asks us, "Do you want to be healed" (John 5:6)?

Consider. Will Jesus ask us to move elsewhere (or will we even listen to Him) if we are unable to sell our house without it being a financial burden? Will God encourage us to begin working at a meaningful non-profit organization if we need to make a corporate salary to maintain our family's living expenses? Will we be able to volunteer our time to a cause the Lord lays upon our hearts if our schedule is so packed that we do not have any available time? Of course, it is rare that such big questions face us. They are more commonly just simple decisions that place undue pressure on us. Have we laid aside *every* weight from our lives—even the small ones—so that we might better discern and respond to what Jesus is doing right now?

I am not looking to tell anyone what those weights, pressures, stresses, anxieties, burdens, demands, or hindrances are in their own life. I entrust that job to God's Spirit, along with everyone's own conscience. Personally speaking, I had to set aside things like running my own business for a time, overcommitting to people, distracting myself with too much digital noise, accumulating unnecessary financial expenses, building up superfluous material excess, eating food that lessened my energy, and more. I remain challenged by this call of Jesus. Just seven months after my trip to the hospital that fateful November, I even lost fifty pounds, uncovering some welcome abdominal muscles underneath my earlier flab. Overall, I am healthy and feeling much lighter now, but fat remains least of the weight that I removed from my life.

If things like these remain stuck to us—or as is often the case, we remain clinging to these burdens—we could easily delay or altogether miss some exciting work God has in store for us, unable to walk forward in liberty. The Lord may still show up and get our attention through a blinding light, a burning bush, a hungry fish, or even a talking donkey (Exodus 3; Numbers 22:22-41; Jonah 1:17-2:10; Acts 9:1-19). In my case, it just took a trip to the hospital. But it doesn't need to take reminders as extreme as these.

The invitation constantly awaits us to rid our lives of anything that gets in the way of doing what Jesus wants us to do right now. There is little telling what that may look like, so let us make ourselves ready in every season. Let's get on the scale, assess our true weight, and drop some pounds.

BUILDING WITH LEGÓ

There I sat in Sacré-Cœur, atop a hill in Paris, staring at a stunning rendition of Jesus. In this French Roman Catholic church, His sacred heart overlooked everyone present, bursting aflame with color. Jesus wasn't the exclusive object that captured my attention, either. Along with thousands of other visitors from around the world, I gazed in wonder at the rest of this incredible white stone basilica. As I kneeled there in the pews, admiring the portrait of Christ and praying with my eyes open, I felt God impress His reality upon me: "This place does not touch the beauty of My true temple."

In the rumble of God's soft yet thunderous breath, my tears flowed. Built over 39 years and visited by travelers from every other nation, how could something as gorgeous as this church not compare to Christ's church? How could something so sacred not touch the hem of the bride's garment? Easy. While the hands and money spent in this massive architecture were more significant than nearly anything we construct today, much like that of the Vatican, the Sistine Chapel, and even Solomon's Temple, this too was built by the hands of mortals.

We may quickly jump to concluding then that it is purely Divine hands which can construct a temple more beautiful than these holy monuments on the Earth. But even this notion falls short of the reality. God does not build primarily with His hands, but with His voice. It was not His hands that went to work on the first day of creation, it was His Word (John 1:1-4). God says "Let," and it is established (Genesis 1:3).

His Word has formed everything we can see and cannot see, including the construction of His house (John 1:1-3). As Jesus promised, "I will build my church" (Matthew 16:18). Even more dramatically, He foretold "I will destroy this temple made with hands, and in three days I will build another made without hands" (Mark 14:58).

There has never been a natural house that has been built entirely without hands. Yet Christ declared that the house God established would not be built with hands. Two specific Greek words are used in the New Testament to relay the concept of "building up" (*oikodomē* and *oikodomēo*), typically translated as "edify" or "edification" today. Unsurprisingly, scripture has lots to say about building up one another using these words (Acts 20:32; Romans 14:19; 15:2; 1 Corinthians 8:1; 10:22; 14:3, 12, 26; Ephesians 4:11-12, 29; 1 Thessalonians 5:13).

As vividly illustrated by a long list of scripture, words are inextricably tied to the building of God's house. In fact, studying the original Greek from which we translate our modern Bibles will lead us to observe another helpful picture that clearly illustrates the importance of our words. The word for "speak" in Greek is one that we may remember well from our childhood playtime: *legō*. Speaking edifying words are the critical building blocks of God's house, eternal phrases and sentences and conversations that strengthen and bind us together as living stones (1 Corinthians 14:26; 1 Peter 2:5).

When we read and quote scripture with others, we are building (2 Timothy 3:16). When we speak the words of Jesus to one another and what it is He reveals to us through His Spirit, we are building (1 Corinthians 14:3, 5, 31). When we share our spiritual gifting with the church, we are building (Ephesians 4:11-12). When we seek to encourage people during despairing times, we are building (1 Thessalonians 5:11-13). When we speak of our love toward one another, we are building (1 Corinthians 8:1). When we extend grace and peace to those in need, we are building (Acts 20:32; Romans 14:19). Enough cannot be highlighted about the power of our words to build up the church of God.

It's not that hard, either. We do not need to wordsmith what we say until it is marked by the perfection of an eloquent public speaker. As Ephesians instructs, "Let no unwholesome word proceed from your mouth, but only such a word as is good for building up, according to the need of the moment, so that it will give grace to those who hear" (Ephesians 4:29, NASB). Just go with the flow of the moment and try to encourage other people. It's that easy. Speaking to others in love and truth is one of the most important aspects of effectively coworking with Jesus, and we have the Spirit of God inside us to make this edifying speech possible.

James writes passionately about the power of our words, starkly warning us how destructive negative words can be. "The tongue is a small part of the body, and yet it boasts of great things. See how great a forest is set aflame by such a small fire! ... With [the tongue] we bless our Lord and Father, and with it we curse men, who have been made in the likeness of God; from the same mouth come both blessing and cursing" (James 3:5-6, 9-10). Clearly, it is far easier to destroy others than build them up.

Of course, while such destructive power should give us serious pause before we speak anything negative, rather than focus solely on the harmful aspects of our words, we can consider what more the tongue is capable of, using positive language instead. Therefore, we can interpret this same passage to read, "The tongue is a small part of the body, and yet it boasts of great things. See how great a [house is built] by such a small member! ... With [the tongue] we bless our Lord and Father, and with it we [build up] men, who have been made in the likeness of God; from the same mouth come both blessing and [building]."

All this is to say, our tongue does more to build the church than our hands can ever do. We are building up one another, God's dwelling place, not a physical building. As beautiful as a white basilica on a Parisian hill may have struck me with my physical eyes, it does not touch the spiritual splendor of God's spotless city on a hill, shining its light to the world that gazes upon her (Matthew 5:14). We only need to exercise our spiritual senses to behold her peerless extravagance. After all, she is—we are—being conformed to His likeness (Romans 8:29).

Unfortunately, we have rather missed this whole point within Christianity. We so casually throw around the encouragement for Christians to "build the kingdom" these days. But let us distinguish what it is that Jesus has called us to exactly so that we do not endeavor to build that which we have not been tasked to build. Put another way, let us understand our actual job description so that we do not try something we have not been given the responsibility or authority to carry out as God's coworkers.

First and foremost, we should distinguish between God's church and His kingdom. While the church is within His kingdom and His kingdom is within us, His church is not the sole territory of His kingdom. Many Christians misunderstand what the kingdom consists of—and I am not saying I have it perfectly figured out either. Still, at the very least, I am confident that we can find God's kingdom wherever the active rule and reign of Jesus Christ is being expressed both in Heaven and on Earth.

When we believe this, a survey of scripture will lead us to learning that the word "building" is never once associated with God's kingdom. Zero mentions. None. Instead, the kingdom is established, sought after, coming, delivered, received, and entered (2 Samuel 7:13, 16; Matthew 6:10; 12:28; Luke 11:2, 20; 17:20; 22:18; 1 Corinthians 15:24; Revelation 12:10). It is preached, proclaimed, and announced as good news (Matthew 4:7, 23; 5:9; 9:35; Luke 4:43; 16:16; Acts 8:12; 28:31). There are keys to it, and it can be taken away or given unto others (Matthew 16:19; 21:43; Mark 4:11; Luke 8:10). While neither here or there, we can be near or far from it, as it even lives within reach and among us, its citizens (Luke 10:9, 11; 17:20-21). Talk alone does not compose it, for the kingdom is a matter of power that the Father is pleased to give His children as a gift (Matthew 19:14; Mark 9:1; Luke 18:16). Clearly, the Bible's selection of verbs and adjectives differs from ours rather dramatically.

If we need new language, we can look to Frank Viola's gripping articulation of the gospel, *Insurgence: Reclaiming the Gospel of the Kingdom*. In this book, he clarifies how believers can help "advance" God's kingdom. I believe this language is better suited to what we mean when we typically speak of "kingdom-building" activities.

For example, Jesus does not teach us to pray, "Please empower me to help build Your kingdom." No. He guides us to ask the Father, "Your kingdom *come*, Your will be done, on Earth as it is in Heaven" (Matthew 6:10). We can do nothing to help build the kingdom or bring it by our own strength. We can only seek the King, working with Him so that He continues to bring His kingdom down for the world to encounter. This is a spiritual work that cannot be completed by using a physical or mental method alone. Should we desire to witness more of the kingdom on Earth, let us humbly do what Jesus encouraged us to do: "Pray then like this" (Matthew 6:9).

As we understand this spiritual reality, finally we will see God's construction taking place before our very eyes. We can stop trying to build the kingdom and start praying that it comes. As we do so, let us also never stop building up one another by continually speaking to each other according to the need of each moment. This sounds a whole lot more comfortable to me than sweating over construction work. It sounds more like walking than running, more like easy than hard, more like nothing than something.

As with everything, we can do nothing apart from Him, and that includes building. Put down the hammer. Start speaking to God and one another. We will marvel at the beauty of His temple.

STAINED HANDS

Christians can be difficult. As much as many believers (my former self included) may be quick to argue with the notion that our responsibility is to do nothing, as soon as good works are mentioned, we will oppose this idea just as fiercely. We race to recite, "For by grace you have been saved through faith. And this is not your own doing; it is the gift of God, *not a result of works*, so that no one may boast" (Ephesians 2:8-9). Nobody will find me arguing with this point, as I hope to have made clear. I cannot boast of anything I have done. His grace bewilders me.

Unfortunately, we too often stop short of the very next verse, selectively referencing only the scripture before it. "For we are His workmanship, created in Christ Jesus *for good works*, which God prepared beforehand, that we should walk in them" (Ephesians 2:10).

Paul reinforces this point further in Philippians. "Therefore, my beloved, as you have always obeyed, so now, not only as in my presence but much more in my absence, work out your own salvation with fear and trembling, for it is God who works in you, both to will *and to work* for His good pleasure" (Philippians 2:12-13).

Paul writes to Titus, too, clearly reminding him that salvation has not come by our own works and righteousness, but because of the grace we have each received. Then he adds, "I want you to insist on these things, so that those who have believed in God may be careful to devote themselves to good works. These things are excellent and profitable for people" (Titus 3:8). The second chapter of James illuminates the importance of good works even more plainly than the apostle Paul does.

As much as we may try to avoid the truth that God has called us into coworking with Him, it is clear throughout the entirety of the New Testament that there is good work, effort, and labor to be done in, by, and unto Christ in response to His magnificent gospel of grace. Though we are not responsible for completing any work apart from Jesus, we still remain accountable to Him for every effort to which He has uniquely called us. In other words, He is responsible for accomplishing the work, while we are accountable for helping Him. He calls, we respond.

But again, I urge everyone in the Spirit—do not mishear or misunderstand this work. This is no work of our own. In the footsteps of Jesus, we are to walk in complete reliance upon His indwelling life, just as He walked in utter dependence upon the life of His Father. We do not work to receive His grace, love, or favor; we work because He has already extended us His grace, love, and favor. There is nothing we can do that God has not done first. Much as we love because He first loved us, our work is simply giving back what Christ gives us in the first place (1 John 4:19).

Still, it seems good works have become something of an unmentionable no-no in evangelicalism these days. We may like the sound of people doing good things, but as soon as these works present themselves to us as opportunities, we quickly categorize them as legalism. If not so extreme, we may respond instead by saying we do not feel "called" to these works, using the spiritual language as some sort of illegitimate exemption.

Even a surface-level study of the Bible will not allow us to remain with our arms crossed to the idea though. In response to the work of Jesus, we are unquestionably called to accomplish good works in partnership with Him (Matthew 5:16; Luke 6:27; Acts 9:36; 2 Corinthians 6:1; 9:8; Colossians 1:10; 2 Thessalonians 2:17; 1 Timothy 2:10; 5:10, 25; 6:18; 2 Timothy 3:16-17; Titus 2:7, 14; 3:14; Hebrews 10:24; James 2:14; 1 Peter 2:12). He beckons us.

In light of everything we have learned to this point, we should not seek out doing good work to feel like we have accomplished something by ourselves. A rich young man made this mistake. Approaching Jesus, he asks, "Teacher, what good deed must I do to have eternal life" (Matthew

19:16)? As much as this man had tried everything, he knew that something was still missing in his life. Even though he had done everything he could on his own, he couldn't figure out why he still didn't feel secure in his pursuit of lasting life.

Jesus responds to the unsatisfied man, saying, "Why do you ask me about what is good? There is only One who is good" (Matthew 19:17). Quite clearly, we cannot do something good to earn anything (Romans 7:18-20). The ultimate Good has already been sent to finish work on our behalf. Anything good we do can exclusively be done because God has empowered us to do it—or has done it for us entirely (1 Peter 4:10-11). This includes every good work that has been prepared for us to walk in because it is His Word which declares what is good in the first place (Genesis 1:31; 2:18).

As much as our good work should feel like no more than steady steps forward in our walk of faith, our hands may regularly ache in accomplishing this work. That's not all, either. We will grow weary. We will sweat. We may bleed. We will even cry. Sleeplessness, blood, sweat, and tears were known by Christ, so why should they not also be known by us (Mark 14:32-42; Luke 22:39-46; John 11:35)?

While we have been called to keep ourselves unstained from the world, remaining in this unblemished spiritual state will often require our hands become quite physically and emotionally stained by the muck and need of this world's inhabitants (James 1:27). Orphans need us.

Widows need us. Refugees and people of color need us. The depressed need us. The disabled need us. The homeless and poor need us. Single parents need us. Divorcees need us. The LGBTQIA+ community need us. Abuse victims need us, as well as its perpetrators. Prisoners need us. Our enemies need us. Those who believe differently than we do need us. And oh God, the religious need us. There is no continent, country, or corner of the world that does not have a need. I know that I am in desperate and daily need.

Together, the church will be corporately presented as a spotless bride to Christ (Isaiah 62:5; 2 Corinthians 11:2; Ephesians 5:25-27; Revelation 19:7-9; 21:2, 9). But the Lord wishes to make our spotlessness visible on the earth today as we roll up our gown's sleeves and get our hands just as dirty as our Groom's. The dirtier the job, the better.

Even the apostle Peter writes, "Baptism, which corresponds to this, now saves you, not as a removal of dirt from the body but as an appeal to God for a good conscience, through the resurrection of Jesus Christ" (1 Peter 3:21). We have not been baptized into Christ so that dirt can be removed from our bodies. We have been baptized into Christ so that we might cowork with God in removing filth from the souls of this world. It is His precious blood and the water of His Word alone that can remove that filth, true. But it is our work with Him that extends His pure invitation to everyone, often offered by our raw, tired hands (Matthew 26:28; John 19:34; Romans 3:25; 5:9; Hebrews 10:4; 1 John 1:7; 5:6-12).

Perhaps it is for this very reason that Jesus spent his early years as a carpenter and artisan. His hands needed preparing for the tireless work they would perform in touching lepers, placing mud on the eyes of the blind, extending love to tax collectors and prostitutes, rejecting the religious and political systems of the day, and becoming stained with His own blood at the self-righteous hands of the sinners He came to save. It is as we allow our own hands to be wounded in service of the Lord and others that we too will help minister His touch within the world.

With Christ, there is no work too difficult, no job too lowly, and no task that shall remain undone. Jesus loves it when we have dirty hands.

THAT'S IMPOSSIBLE

I'm a sucker for movies. There's no film too old, black and white, silent, enigmatic, bad, or just plain weird for my tastes. I love the craft and all that it can convey through the art of story, sight, and sound. I am an oddity in the movies I like to watch, though. As beautiful as I find the cinematic arts, people rarely buy tickets at the box office to watch characters accomplish basic, normal, everyday feats. It would be difficult to think of a movie trailer that bombastically promotes a film in which its protagonists overcome *surmountable* odds.

In other words, we love when stories consist of impossible feats, even tales which no one can readily explain. The stories that live on in their telling over generations involve slaying unbeatable enemies, witnessing unexplainable events, venturing into mystical territory, and overcoming insurmountable challenges. They sound a lot like the type of stories that Jesus likes telling, too.

God is not in the business of weaving narratives that involve the possible, even the plausible. He is looking to tell one true, magnificent, eternal, impossible story that solely points to the God who makes all things possible. As Jesus puts plainly, "With man it is impossible, but not with God. For all things are possible with God" (Mark 10:27).

Why is it then that we routinely set out to accomplish work that can be done in our own strength? If we truly believe in the power of Jesus Christ and the truth that His Spirit indwells us at this very moment, why would we not enlist ourselves for the impossible work (Isaiah 6:8)? He wants us to move mountains, not molehills (Matthew 17:20).

I regret to say that this has been a pattern in my own life. As much as I love watching impossible stories on the silver screen, I have not counted myself as a key character in the unfolding narrative of Christ. I have made myself an audience member who sits comfortably in the darkness of the theatre rather than engaging as a leading actor magnified by the projector's light. My Director invites me to walk into His extraordinary story, but I commonly choose to sit myself out, in the ordinary. In fact, there is an open casting call, and we have each been granted walk-on roles should we accept His generous, continuous invitation.

Yes, as I look back on the work of my hands, I have opted into doing things for God that I know I can accomplish on my own. "That's doable," I think to myself. When it's doable, I do it. As much as I have done lots, the lots that I have done honestly amounts to very little. I do not dream big enough with Jesus, letting my petty ideas needlessly squash the profound ones He has dreamt up for me.

The Lord invites us into the undoable. The greatest work I can truly attest to having contributed toward over my lifetime is work that I cannot take any credit for personally. Yes, I responded to the call of God and believed that He was up to something in those instances, but the lasting impact of any work I have set my hand to is not at all my own accomplishment. It is His accomplishment. I am just a supporting character to the Hero of this story.

This does not mean that impossible work necessitates everything we do amount to a huge work, either. Sometimes, it is rather small (Zechariah 4:10). In fact, I would say it is predominantly small. But it remains His work, nonetheless. Impossible work has nothing to do with the perceivable size of it. It may even remain invisible to our own eyes. His work often begins as tiny and seemingly insignificant as a mustard seed, but we should never scoff at their small beginnings (Zechariah 4:10; Mark 4:30-32). God loves starting with individuals, families, and remnants, always causing the growth Himself (Genesis 45:7; Zechariah 8:12; Acts 15:17; Romans 1:15; 1 Corinthians 3:6-7).

I don't want to do anything that feels possible anymore. I want to wait for the impossible. When I truly believe, "I can't do it," that's when I know Jesus is up to something grand. Of course, as we already discussed, we should all affirm that even our breathing in this very moment would not be possible without God. But I confess that it feels difficult to consider my breathing impossible at times, as much as I may try to do so. I take my physical abilities for granted. Until our essential human functions have been stripped away, that is typically what we all do.

Framed from another angle, I can say that it is exclusively when I have professed my weakness that the important work has been best accomplished. Paul explained this phenomenon. In an exchange with the Lord through prayer, the apostle expresses, "[Jesus] has said to me, 'My grace is sufficient for you, for power is perfected in weakness.' Most gladly, therefore, I will rather boast about my weaknesses, so that the power of Christ may dwell in me" (2 Corinthians 12:9). Strength fails, while weakness wins.

It is rare that we find people boasting in their downfalls these days. Even in the church, there is so much encouragement for us to focus on our strengths. Though there remains some practicality to this psychological principle, it is not a principle the Lord has given to us. He says that His power is perfected in our weakness. The Bible exhorts us to express our failings and our faults. Yet many of us are so quick to ramble on about our good sides, our strong suits, and our noteworthy achievements.

If even Jesus professed His inability to do anything without His Father, why shouldn't we follow in His footsteps (John 5:30)? If the apostle Paul did not consider himself great, why shouldn't we also consider ourselves least of all (Ephesians 3:8)? This is not to say we should venture into self-loathing or consider less of ourselves, but we should absolutely consider ourselves less. The more we regularly boast in our weakness, the more God's greatness might be dramatically displayed for everyone to see. As the gospel says, "He must increase, but I must decrease" (John 3:30).

When we say, "I can't do that" is when God steps in to say that He can. When we say "I'm not able," that is when He says He is. Even when *we aren't, we can't,* and *we couldn't,* God is continually proving, *I AM, I can,* and *I will.*

Let us each lay aside our attempts to do anymore possible, meaningless, and boring work. We serve a God of the impossible. Let us join Him on the screen as an underdog in the story He continues directing. He has quite the ending in mind.

QUESTION
How do I work with Jesus?

ANSWER
Walk.

READ
Ephesians 2:10

REFLECT
- Have you felt the necessity to run at an unsustainable pace? How has reading this helped you consider slowing down?
- What are the weights in your life that keep getting in the way of your walk of faith? How will you take action to lay those aside?
- How has your perspective on building now changed? Where will you be praying for the kingdom to come in your world?
- Have you had an aversion or heard others avoid doing "good works?" Where can you begin to get your hands dirty with God?
- Did you know you are a character in God's story? What impossible work do you feel called to by Jesus, but nervous about starting?

WHAT IS GOD'S PLAN FOR ME?

*And I am sure of this, that He who began
a good work in you will bring it to completion
at the Day of Jesus Christ.*
Philippians 1:6

ADJUSTING TIMELINES

"**M**an plans and God laughs." Or so the old Yiddish proverb goes. The facts are not lost on any of us—life rarely turns out how we expect. Our mortal lives may not end as we initially hope. They are each full of surprising twists and turns, progress and setbacks, adventure and peril. We gain, and we lose. We succeed, and we fail. We live, and we die. As our experience carries on over seasons, years, and decades, it becomes difficult to predict, let alone plan for. The human experience can feel frustrating.

Still, we shouldn't be so quick to presume what the Divine finds comedic. Though we may repeat adages like this as an innocent attempt to comfort ourselves amid life's unpredictability, God never laughs at our plans. He knows—and cares—about our plans as intimately as we do. In fact, it is very likely that Jesus originally placed many of those plans into our hearts (Ezekiel 36:26; Ecclesiastes 3:11).

Solomon agrees, noting, "The heart of man plans his way, but the Lord establishes his steps" (Proverbs 16:9). The wise king did not say that the Lord discards our plans for His own, laughing at what we set out to do with ourselves. He is a compassionate Father who knows us, listens to us, and hopes for our very best. Remembering that we can do nothing apart from Him, He is the One who makes it possible for us to even consider and accomplish these plans in the first place. Jesus seeks to help our footsteps along the path He has us each walking. He prepares our way so that the best possible plans might eventually be accomplished in harmonious concert with Him.

True, our plans do not always line up with God's best. Our ambitions are often selfish and we set ourselves on a course of destruction that doesn't consider the bigger picture. We are limited in our scope of understanding and realization of possibility. The prophet Jeremiah says that our hearts can be misguided, deceptive in fact (Jeremiah 17:9-10). But we regularly misread and misunderstand scripture, throwing out the figurative baby with the bathwater. "If our hearts are deceptive," we reason, "then I better learn to detest my heart and disregard its plans." But the Lord does not want us to despise ourselves or ignore our hearts. He invites us to delight in Him and learn the desires of a new heart. His heart (Psalm 37:4).

Throughout history, Jesus has been known to do away with initial, temporary orders so that He might bring about second, permanent ones (1 Corinthians 15:45; Hebrews 10:9). Studying the whole of Jeremiah's prophesies, we would realize this. God doesn't condemn everybody's desires or plans. He just commands we not trust ourselves. As the servant proclaims, "Cursed is the man who trusts in man and makes flesh his strength, whose heart turns away from the Lord... Blessed is the man who trusts in the Lord, whose trust is the Lord" (Jeremiah 17:5, 7).

As we trust in the Lord and allow Him to become our greatest desire, we can also shout with the psalmist, "May [God] grant you your heart's desire and fulfill all your plans" (Psalm 20:4)! Christ has poured out His very Spirit within our hearts, complete with extravagant plans (2 Corinthians 1:22). As impossibly daunting as those plans may at times feel, He wants us to realize them just as much as we want to realize them, if not more so. In fact, He is already at work on our behalf to help us accomplish them (Isaiah 46:10; 55:10; Jeremiah 23:20).

Though we may continually need to be reminded of this, He is on a mission with us to accomplish something of significant and lasting effect over the course of our walks. He has eternal purposes in mind (Romans 8:28; Ephesians 1:9-10; 3:11-12). Moreover, He is for us, not against us (Romans 8:31). Jeremiah reinforces this point, again. "For I know the plans I have for you, declares the Lord, plans for welfare and not for evil, to give you a future and a hope" (Jeremiah 29:11).

May we never forget that we are coworkers with the Lord. Partners help one another accomplish shared plans, with an eye always towards the future. As such, our Christ-centered plans—even the plans we may feel primarily benefit us—are now shared plans. His plans become ours. And our plans begin to look an awful lot like His. The will of God eventually aligns to become our will (Psalm 40:8; 143:10). The plans we have for ourselves shift and shake until gold emerges in the pan.

Though Jesus may deprive us of our own plans being fulfilled momentarily, I have observed He typically does this so that He can fulfill what we don't yet know we *truly* want and need to accomplish. Eventually, we discover the pearls of great price that are worth sacrificing everything for, and then He brings us to the altar of sacrifice (Matthew 13:44-46). The plans we hold either fade away like dust, helping us realize their inconsequence, or they grow without any of our own effort, revealing those that were forged to last by the Original Planner.

I know a brother in the Lord who carries a worrisome misunderstanding in this regard. As sincerely zealous as he is for Jesus, he regularly criticizes his human heart. Rather than see his heart and its plans as a good thing, he largely views it as wicked, calling it his "wanter." I was confused when I first heard this phrase, unsure what he meant, but he quickly explained himself to me. He calls his heart a wanter "because it wants things." As if that is evil.

Jesus Christ has wants of His own—He wants every last bit of us. In fact, the Son felt free to regularly confess and ask His Father to meet His wants, even when He knew His desires may not align with God's will (Matthew 26:39; Mark 14:36; Luke 22:42; John 17:24). We have not primarily because we ask not (James 4:3). Indeed, it is the Spirit who tests our hearts, but not every test will return a negative response (Jeremiah 17:10). God is constantly conforming us into His likeness, including our wants into His wants. We don't need to throw away the hopes and dreams the Lord has placed within us. In fact, He won't let us.

The problem lies not with our hearts or our plans in and of themselves. God is not sitting up in heaven callously laughing at the things we hope to do. The main problem lies with our timelines. Accordingly, the more appropriate adage would express, "Man schedules his plans, and God schedules otherwise."

Scripture tells us that 1,000 years is like one day to God, but also that one day is like 1,000 years (2 Peter 3:8). This means that Jesus has a very long-term perspective in mind. Christians will often glibly encourage we maintain an "eternal perspective." That may feel difficult to do and impractical though.

I just think we should all find it quite comforting that the Lord does not only experience 1,000 years like a day, but He also considers each day like 1,000 years. This reinforces the truth that Christ is fulfilling His plan with such precision in the microscopy of this moment that His concern for today cannot be overstated. He cares about the big picture, absolutely, but He will do everything He can in the small moments to bring His big picture plan to pass. His Spirit works both in microseconds and millenniums.

When we study the lives of predecessors in the faith, there is none in which the Lord accomplished everything they wanted—or even He wanted—in mere moments. It was always a process. Abraham waited twenty-five years before his son, Isaac, was born. Joseph waited twenty-two years to see his dream fulfilled and embrace his family again. Moses spent forty years in Midian before being called back to lead his people out of Egypt. David waited over twenty years from the time of his anointing to becoming king over the entire nation of Israel. Jesus Himself waited thirty years before His ministry began. The apostle Paul waited fourteen years between his radical conversion and his first missionary trip with Barnabas. And this is just a highlight reel. Throughout the whole of scripture and our own experience, the evidence is clear: God works while we wait. In fact, He even does it when we are off the clock, fast asleep (Psalm 127:2, NASB).

There has never been one word delivered by Jesus which He has not brought to pass in His flawless timing. Even if we feel something He promised still hasn't manifested yet, we should remain assured that it will happen, without a doubt. God's calendar doesn't cover just days, months, and years, but decades, generations, and centuries. We serve a God who never tires or becomes deterred from His goals.

If it's any consolation, we're not alone in our waiting. We can find many promises that our forefathers never saw take place while they remained present in their earthly tents (2 Corinthians 5:1). Abraham never saw his descendants number the stars (Genesis 15:5-6). David never saw the everlasting kingdom be established (2 Samuel 7:12-17). Prophet after prophet never saw the Messiah come in His fullness (Matthew 13:17). Even recently I heard Billy Graham and Dennis Rainey share stories about their fathers and grandfathers being delivered words which went unrealized in a single generation. But even these were absolutely realized in the ministries the Lord eventually established through them, just one or two generations later.

I have a similar, unconcluded story myself. Many years ago, while my first two children were still very young, my wife and I found ourselves deep in prayer late into the night. Over the course of the evening, I secretly prayed to the Lord, asking Him to answer one of my foremost desires. My heart longed to know that all my children, grandchildren, and heritage to follow my wife and me would know and love the Lord Jesus above every other thing in this world. Tears soaked my bedsheets as I fervently offered up the words, my heart pounding in passionate request.

The next day, I received an unexpected call from a brother in Christ who lived across the country, Donald. Without prompting, he began to share very boldly with me that whatever it was I prayed to Jesus the night before, the Father had heard loud and clear. Moreover, according to what he was discerning in the Spirit, Donald resolutely confirmed, "It will happen." I was undone.

Obviously, by the very nature of this request, I will not see it answered over the course of my mortal life. If I'm honest, it feels risky to even commit this story to writing. But I trust the Word of the Lord. Even if down the road I may witness my children or grandchildren struggling in their walks of faith, I have already committed to trust in this promise of God and that He will seek, save, and keep them. My heritage with Nicole will know and love Jesus above every other thing, praise Him.

It may feel unhelpful, even a little freaky to say that we have eternity to see every plan of ours and the Lord's come to pass. We may grow frustrated in the here and now, but God is dealing with us in the there and later, too. Even as the edges of our life in these failing bodies are constrained, Christ's life and activity are not. The Bible promises, "I am sure of this, that He who began a good work in you will bring it to completion at the Day of Jesus Christ" (Philippians 1:6). 100% of the time, we can rest assured that God's Word will happen. His record is flawless. And it will remain flawless.

Such wholehearted belief was the very basis of Abraham's righteousness (Genesis 15:5-6; Romans 4:3; Galatians 3:6; James 2:23). We can join a great number of witnesses in believing the Lord even before His promises may be realized (Hebrews 12:1). As our hall of forerunners testifies, "All these died in faith, without receiving the promises, but having seen them and having welcomed them from a distance" (Hebrews 11:13). We should similarly let our faith go the distance with Christ.

Yes, our plans will probably take longer than we expect before they are completed, but then again, they may be accomplished suddenly. In the book, *The Release of the Spirit*, Watchman Nee puts it this way, "The Lord employs two different means to break our outward man. One is gradual. The other is sudden. To some, the Lord gives a sudden breaking, followed by a gradual one. With others, the Lord arranges constant daily trials, until one day He brings about a large-scale breaking. If it is not the sudden first and then the gradual, then it is the gradual followed by the sudden. It would seem the Lord usually spends several years upon most of us before He can accomplish this work of breaking. The timing is in His hand. We cannot shorten the time, though we certainly can prolong it."

I can confirm that this has proven quite true in my own life. Brother Nee's insight further reinforces the principle that God cares much more about what He wants to do *in* us than what He wants to do for us or even through us. Do our plans prioritize what we will accomplish, or our conformation to Christ's glorious likeness? Jesus is extremely concerned with the latter, while we concentrate exorbitantly on the former.

When it comes to our plans, we can stop tapping our feet and staring at our watches. What we can pray for more of in the interim is patience (Galatians 5:22-23). Fortunately, His Spirit is producing that patience in each of us as we abide in Him, even when we may not be privy to the fruit's sometimes slow-growing presence. Don't worry, He has not gone anywhere. He remains very much at work, producing His endurance within us as we wait. As Solomon writes, "Better is the end of a thing than its beginning, and the patient in spirit is better than the proud in spirit" (Ecclesiastes 7:8).

Though we should still surrender our individual plans to the Lord, He will often turn the ash of our heart's sacrifice into beauty beyond description, making something more of it than we can imagine (Isaiah 61:3). Jesus knows our detailed wants and grandest plans; they are not invisible or unimportant to Him as we choose to follow Him (Psalm 37:4-5). He also knows our most intimate needs; He will meet them all (Matthew 6:7-8). More than anything, God knows our most exquisite end; He will help establish our steps until we arrive there, even carrying us forward if He must (Psalm 37:23; Proverbs 16:9; Isaiah 46:3-4).

Jesus has a destination in mind for each one of us that supersedes any possible expectation or hope that we could possibly maintain for ourselves. We may not necessarily see it realized exactly as we plan on our own, but God works in methods that exceed our wildest estimations when viewed with His perspective.

As one of my best friends, Evan, says, "If it's too good to be true, it probably *is* true with the Lord." I'm not talking about Santa Clause or pixie dust. The conclusion that God has in store for every one of us will pulverize any plan we could possibly write for ourselves. The plans we have made on our own will end up paling in comparison to His plans.

Similarly, the plans He establishes in us will be realized beyond every best-case scenario we can dream up alone. He will finish every good work He has begun in us. He is the Finisher, the Completer, the Omega, and the End (Hebrews 12:2; Revelation 22:13). We can bet on it. On Him. Every plan the Lord shares with us will be accomplished in Christ Jesus. Full stop.

This is not hyperbole. Scripture tells us, "For all the promises of God find their Yes in Him. That is why it is through Him that we utter our Amen to God for His glory" (2 Corinthians 1:20). Though it may be challenging for doers like us, we probably just need to reset our clocks and relinquish our calendars, stepping back a bit to take in the whole picture. It's bigger than we could possibly imagine. As a result, it may also require a good deal more time than we would plan for ourselves. Personally, I hate waiting, but He's always worth waiting for.

We may think that God is laughing at us and the plans we have carried in our hearts for so long, but we are mistaken. In truth, He's just smiling at us, guiding our every step of the way until completed. Jesus finishes absolutely everything He begins. Yes. Amen.

AGELESS FAITHFUL

When we see marriages that enjoy decades of fidelity and love, we call those spouses faithful. When we have friends who stick with us through thick and thin over a long period of time, we call them faithful. When we care for pets who serve as long-lasting, furry companions, we call them faithful. Even geysers in the ground that regularly spout up water we have bestowed congenial names like Old Faithful. As much as we may value faithfulness, though, our earthly pictures of faithfulness lack substance.

Fortunately, we have a God in heaven who offers us a very different, incredibly substantial picture of faithfulness (Colossians 2:17). Indeed, He defines fidelity and love. He is the greatest friend. He is the most loyal. And He is always on time.

In short, Jesus never fails. He never has failed us, and He never will fail us. God is the true Faithful One. In fact, it's not only that He began His faithfulness streak a couple thousand years ago. For eternity, God has remained the same. Yesterday, today, and tomorrow, there is no change in Him (Hebrews 13:8). He fulfills His word, every time (Proverbs 30:5; Luke 1:20; 24:44). He is beyond old and faithful, for He is the Ageless Faithful.

Regrettably, we can still tend toward accusing Jesus of unfaithfulness—even if quietly in our hearts. Though our own faithfulness still lacks any comparison to God's, what if our spouses accused us of adultery after remaining wholly true to our vows? What if our friends distanced themselves from us and accused us of not caring for them, even if that were not the case? Can we imagine anything as hurtful as this?

Despite this, His heart never changes toward us. Jesus has us on His mind and in His sight always, making even the worst of circumstances turn out for our good (Genesis 50:20). Again, we need to recalibrate our definitions of faithfulness, for our paltry understandings of it do not scratch the surface of our God.

One reason we may feel frequently tempted to callously consider the Ageless Faithful unfaithful or untrue rarely lies in what we see Jesus doing, but in our expectations of what He *will* do. In my parents' ministry to countless married couples, they often say, "Expectations are relationship killers." How true. We have misinterpreted God's promises, establishing expectations upon Him and resenting Him when He does not meet them exactly as we demand. We have centered the purposes of God around ourselves rather than around Him.

As we reviewed earlier, we so often believe God wants to do something for us. But He begins that work inside of us. Christ's work addresses the whole person, not just a singular aspect of our lives. We brashly demand Him to answer our material desires, and yet He begins with our spiritual needs. We ask for God to give us more money, and yet He has already granted us all the riches there are to be found (Mark 6:19-20; 10:21; Mark 10:21; Luke 12:33; 18:22; Ephesians 3:7-8; Philippians 4:19; Colossians 1:27; 2:2; 3:24; Hebrews 11:26; 1 Peter 1:7). We hope for deeper relationships, and yet He has given us the most precious of relationships in Christ and His family (Romans 8:19, 23; Galatians 4:5; Ephesians 1:5). We beg for more favor in our human work, and yet the Father looks upon every one of us with the very same eyes with which He looks upon His Son, Jesus, seated at His right hand (Luke 2:40, 52; Ephesians 2:5-7; Colossians 3:1; Hebrews 12:2).

To understand this further, we should distinguish between the two types of promises that the Lord delivers. First are His written promises. These are the many, general words of God that we can find delivered in scripture, inerrant and profitable for our training in righteousness (2 Timothy 3:16). Every one of these words points to the true and incarnate Word, which is Christ. Throughout the Bible's pages, we will discover the promise of Jesus that has been made visible and dispersed to everyone who believes in Him. Every letter of scripture is true, end of story. We can take hold of every biblical promise to the church at large as our very own (Hebrews 6:13-20; 10:23).

Another type of promise God delivers us is through His spoken word. These are the few, specific words of God that He delivers to us individually through His Holy Spirit. Every word spoken to us, when heard rightly and spiritually weighed, is also true (Proverbs 30:5; 1 Corinthians 14:30-32; 1 Thessalonians 5:21). The real question that needs answering with such words is whether it is Jesus who declared them, or if we have heard one of the many other voices constantly clamoring for our attention. Often, portions of these spoken words are true, but not all of it is true (1 Thessalonians 5:19-21). Again, we need discernment. Of course, it should go without saying that a good word will never contradict God's written word (2 Corinthians 11:14-15).

Even the written word of God is lifeless without the spoken word (John 5:39-40). As A.W. Tozer writes in *The Pursuit of God*, "The Bible will never be a living Book to us until we are convinced that God is articulate in His universe... A man may say, 'These words are addressed to me,' and yet in his heart not feel and know that they are. He is the victim of a divided psychology. He tries to think of God as mute everywhere else and vocal only in a book." May we never mute the voice of our God.

In both these words, written and spoken, many and few, general and specific, we should reevaluate what God is really trying to communicate. Even as I have personally exercised discernment so that I might better hear Jesus, I frequently misunderstand what He is precisely trying to do. He has not only given us ears to hear, though—He has granted us His mind (1 Corinthians 2:16).

Many years ago, a pastor named Dennis felt compelled to stop mid-sermon and prophesy over me one Sunday morning at my local church. Having participated in that community for many years, everyone should know as a caveat that this was not a regular occurrence; I remember just one other time this happened in over four years. Still, my pastor at the time felt prompted by the Holy Spirit to stop everything and deliver this word to me.

"Whoa," Dennis began as if being suddenly struck by something large. "You are going to be very rich." He looked me in the eye long and hard to convey the weight of what he was sharing, then proceeded forward with his sermon to the entire congregation.

Now, I realize this is a word that many Christians might skeptically—and rightfully—question. I would, too, given its similitude to a misinformed prosperity gospel; but this was no mega church that preached words which tickled the ears (2 Timothy 4:3-4, NASB). As he shared it, I felt overwhelming confirmation in my spirit. I was not surprised by the word. I knew it was true and Dennis was not the one who spoke it, he simply conveyed it as God's vessel.

One year later, I sold my first startup in an all-stock transaction that was valued at a healthy amount, but nothing extravagant out of the gate. I held onto the stock for many years and, over time (by none of my own effort, I might add) it grew to become worth millions of dollars. This value was substantiated by the fact that three Fortune 100 companies made offers to purchase my parent company. Still, my equity remained only paper, nothing more. In other words, it wasn't "liquid," which is a fancy way of saying it still wasn't money in the bank.

Despite having turned down those substantial acquisition attempts previously, the parent company I had sold mine to eventually reached an unfortunate cash position. Though on paper I was worth millions, the company I partly owned ended up selling for an amount that led my fortune in equity to become worth…*wait for it*…nothing. $0. Goose egg. Wallpaper was worth more than my stock certificates.

As much as I did not let emotions overwhelm me, most people should easily be able to imagine my disappointment. It was like I had a winning lottery ticket in my wallet for seven years, just waiting to be cashed out, and then it evaporated. Gone in an instant.

My nine-year-old son, Tolan, was driving somewhere with me shortly after I was made aware of the transaction's finality and had discussed it with Nicole. Recognizing that his mom and I were discouraged, my son asked what had happened. Avoiding any unnecessary details, I solemnly summarized, "Something that was worth a lot is no longer worth anything. But that's okay, money isn't everything."

Sitting there next to me on the drive to our destination, he smiled peacefully in response. Without a moment's hesitation, Tolan sublimely answered, "I know. We have untold riches of love stored up for us." Out of the mouths of babes.

The Lord is so kind in His provision. While I could have grown deeply frustrated by this event, wounded even, declaring God to be unfaithful to His word, as I survey my life, I am unfathomably rich. What do I want for that I do not already have? What treasure is not already stored away for me, hidden with Christ in God (Colossians 3:3)? All things belong to me in the Person of Jesus (1 Corinthians 3:21-23, NASB). I do not say that as an intangible Christian platitude. I believe it. My father, too, regularly declares how very rich he is—on the meager salary of a missionary. And I agree, my parents are rich beyond measure.

I am not here to say that there is no earthly prosperity to be had in Christ Jesus. For some, there is. For many, there isn't. For many others, there shouldn't be, as money remains an obstacle to many entering the kingdom of God (1 Timothy 6:10; Hebrews 13:5). All I know for me is what I felt soon after this event. In my spirit, I settled, "This makes sense." Why would I ever want to reach a place where I am not reliant upon the provision of the Lord? Why would I want to enjoy a lifestyle in which I am not dependent upon the storehouses of my God (Malachi 3:10)? Why would I seek any inheritance other than that which is promised to the poor in spirit (Matthew 5:3)?

As I think about the word that my pastor declared over me all those years ago, who is to say that the riches the Lord spoke over me is the wealth many might have interpreted? On the other hand, who is to say that Jesus is done with me, either? He may give me more in a financial sense. Or, I may even end up with less than I have currently. Paul learned how to be content in any circumstance (Philippians 4:11-13). Like him, I will choose to be grateful, too. For I have been granted true wealth, and that treasure can solely be discovered in Christ Jesus (Hebrews 11:26). Anything I end up gaining in this world is His in the first place, and I desire nothing more than to return it back to Him.

Whatever the outcome of my life and my plans, God is faithful. He speaks only truth. While we may not yet see things tangibly, He will accomplish everything He promises. He who began a good work in us—in me—will be faithful to complete it. The riches we tend to believe are better here and now do not compare to the riches He has stored up for us forever, as my young son already understands well beyond his years. We should each reframe and rethink what prosperity means in the kingdom of God.

Behold, the Ageless Faithful. As faithful as the sun rises, as sure as the foundations of the world, as consistent as gravity, there is none like our God. Our earthly definitions of faithfulness will not suffice. "The saying is trustworthy … 'if we are faithless, He remains faithful—for He cannot deny Himself" (2 Timothy 2:11, 13).

Through the ups and downs of his life, after years of time in the wilderness running for his life from the hands of King Saul, David finally saw the promises of the Lord coming to pass as he became king over all of Israel (2 Samuel 5:1-10). In witnessing this act of great faithfulness, after twenty-two years of waiting, it is believed that the psalmist specifically scribed, "The Lord will fulfill His purpose for me; Your steadfast love, O Lord, endures forever. Do not forsake the work of Your hands" (Psalm 138:3).

With our forefather in the faith, we can agree. It is not just that Jesus *will not* forsake the work of His hands; He *cannot*. Independent of anything we have done, are doing, or will do, He does it for us.

DAY FOUR

"**L**ord, if you had been here, my brother would not have died" (John 11:32). These were the disappointed, brokenhearted words of both Mary and Martha after Lazarus passed away. But if we inspect these words more closely, we may find ourselves speaking them.

Earlier, the sisters had sent word to Jesus of Lazarus' condition, fully believing that Christ could—and would—heal him (John 11:3). They had already seen Jesus work healing after healing, so why would He not work another one for a friend He truly loved? Jesus responded, "This illness does not lead to death. It is for the glory of God, so that the Son of God may be glorified through it" (John 11:4).

We should each be able to imagine, at least slightly, how these dear sisters may have quickly interpreted these words of Jesus to mean that Lazarus would not die. And yet, by all earthly interpretations, their brother did die. Their family mourned. They wrapped him in linen cloth and laid his body in a cave. Jesus didn't even show up at the funeral, what would be considered an outrageous social offense at the time.

When Jesus eventually did appear in Bethany and told Martha that Lazarus would rise again, she responded with the very best her heart could offer, trusting in the future promises of God. Through tears, she concedes, "I know that [Lazarus] will rise again in the resurrection on the last day" (John 11:24).

I recognize myself in these aching words. In the face of disappointment, when my plans have felt dashed and my hope extinguished, I try to muster up every last morsel of faith that I can in the face of my precious Lord. I rely on what I know will eventually happen, someday, rather than hoping in what God wants to show me in the moment, today. I say, "I know that You will do what You say," but what I really mean to say is, "Why didn't You do what I asked You now?"

The fact is, Jesus often doesn't show up when, or even how, we might predict. He is unfailing, but He is also unpredictable (Psalm 77:1-12, NLT). I cannot explain it fully. None of us can. But what Christ declared to the sisters before Lazarus died remains just as true today. "It is for the glory of God, so that the Son of God may be glorified through it" (John 11:4). When we die, He can live. When we fail, He can succeed. When we are weak, He is strong. When we do nothing, He can do something.

During the life of Jesus, the Jewish people believed that the human soul remained in the general vicinity of its body for three days after death, somewhat lost and confused between death and before burial. Because of this, they performed *shemira*, which represented a religious ritual of guarding a body before burial. Not yet having witnessed the resurrection of Jesus, this was a belief and custom that Mary, Martha, and their Jewish relatives would have likely held to as well.

Let us imagine their hopes for just a moment. Perhaps the sisters prayed for Lazarus at first. But, as his condition worsened, they were eventually compelled to send for Jesus. After hearing that this sickness would not lead unto death from their Rabbi, surely they would have praised God. Momentarily, that is. For as their brother's condition worsened, they probably grew very puzzled over what Jesus said. As Lazarus took his dying breaths, they could have easily questioned the truth of God's word, as it did not align with what they were seeing (John 11:37).

But even then, at their endpoint, can we not imagine them praying one last time? "Yahweh, please send Yeshua to heal my brother before his soul departs." They waited, desperate for an answer. One day passed. Then a second. The sun rose again, but it set just as quickly. By midnight on the third day, any remaining hope to spend time with their brother on this Earth was finally buried with him. Darkness fell.

We are so eager for the Lord to show up, but we must realize that our God does not deal within the confines of our own limitations. Even as we might believe, "You can heal, fix, and solve" whatever situation faces us, we often place stipulations on how or when God can accomplish that work. But our God is not limited by what has happened over time, in our circumstances, or even in death itself. He is most certainly not constrained to working within our stipulations.

As we were already reminded, Jesus is the God of the impossible. Anything we can imagine could be accomplished by Him. In fact, everything we *can't* imagine could be accomplished by Him. He can do anything. Just as we can do nothing apart from Him.

As Jesus told Mary that fateful day, even while the body of Lazarus remained in a pitch black cave, "I am the Resurrection and the Life. Whoever believes in Me, though he die, yet shall he live, and everyone who lives and believes in Me shall never die. Do you believe this" (John 11:25-26)? Jesus is not purely asking if we believe that we will live forever as we trust in Him. He is asking—and continues asking—whether we believe that He is the God of resurrection power who can do anything and everything beyond the limitations of this world and its natural laws. He is *the* Resurrection. Do we believe He can resurrect our dying relationships, plans, and projects? Maybe they're already dead, even.

Jesus still asks, "Do you believe this?" Do we really? Can He do it? Will He?

Most of us already know the end of this story. Lazarus did not remain stuck in a gloomy cave, stinking in his bandages, rotting away after his soul left his body. Jesus showed up. He did not arrive when Mary and Martha expected. He didn't even appear when they had asked. But He did burst onto the scene when all hope seemed lost.

Even though our hopes may wither on day three, our God still answers on day four, at the thirteenth hour, and after the rooster crows (Matthew 26:34, 75; John 21:7). He is moved with compassion on our behalf, weeping with us (John 11:33-35). We serve the God of resurrection, unconstrained to finishing His work even as we mourn over the losses in our lives. It is through such mourning that the Lord's truest power can be placed on display for all to behold in awe (Psalm 30:11; Jeremiah 31:13).

When we finally give up, Jesus breaks in to rescue, redeem, repurpose, renew, and resurrect. As limited as our own hope may then feel, hanging on by a mere thread, we would be wise to heed scripture's exhortation, "Let us hold fast the confession of our hope without wavering, for He who promised is faithful" (Hebrews 10:23).

As our great High Priest, Jesus cries out with a loud voice before the throne even now, interceding on our behalf, "Father, I thank You that You have heard Me. I knew that You always hear Me, but I said this on account of the people standing around, that they may believe that You sent Me ... Lazarus, come out" (John 11:41-43).

Lazarus rose again. More importantly, Christ did. Just as we, too, will rise again with Him (1 Corinthians 15:12-23; 2 Corinthians 4:13-14; 1 Thessalonians 4:16). Though our time in the cave may feel disagreeably dank and over-whelmingly dark, the light on the other side will astound us. He has already overcome the grave, just as He plans to overcome every grave in our own lives for the sake of God's glory (Romans 6:3-11). It may not happen how we ask or expect, but we can take Him at His word. This "does not lead to death" (John 11:4).

THE UNBELIEVABLE UNSEEN

When I was a teenager, I took it upon myself to catch up with all the great movies that had come before me. So, one night after a late shift I drove to my local Blockbuster. That evening, I rented the VHS release of *The Shawshank Redemption*. Believing that the best stories all point to one Story, I starkly remember my reaction to the film even at this exact moment. I was captivated. I cried with joy even.

While I hate to spoil things for anyone who has still not seen the masterpiece, its theme centers on hope. Andy Dufresne, the main character portrayed by Tim Robbins, clearly summarizes, "Remember… hope is a good thing, maybe the best of things, and no good thing ever dies." The final climax of this story moved me so profoundly that I had to rewind and re-watch the last fifteen minutes three times. It was nearly 1:30 AM as I first finished the movie, but it didn't matter. I had to see it again. And again. And again.

Decades after its original release, there's a reason the film still enjoys its cultural popularity. Hope is something we all long for. Humanity craves it. We want to hope for the best. But, wounded by life's disappointments and our personal pile of failures, we distance ourselves from living in such experience. We grow to believe it's childish, ignorant, even foolish to hope for anything. As Morgan Freeman's Red, the film's other main character, cynically points out, "Let me tell you something, my friend. Hope is a dangerous thing. Hope can drive a man insane."

With a worldly perspective, Red is right. But with God's perspective, he's not. I am not just suggesting we try keeping a positive mental attitude in the present. I am talking about hoping in what God has planned for us as His children, both now *and* later. What's the best thing we could possibly hope for at the end of our lives? As we consider what a life well-lived looks like and what Jesus has in store for us, how would we describe it? How far will we let our hope extend?

Our wildest imagination does not touch the hem of Christ's plans for us. The borders of our minds cannot fathom the boundlessness of His eternal glory and immeasurable love. We prefer understanding and clarity, but with God, mystery is more common which, by its very definition, cannot be described. Words crumble under the weight

of such glory. Even heavenly visions cannot express t[...]
fullness or greatness of His purposes for us.

Still, the Lord wants us to hope with Him (1 Cor[...]
thians 13:13). Defined, we know that "faith is the ass[...]
ance of things hoped for, the conviction of things not se[...]
(Hebrews 10:23). It is difficult to feel conviction for t[...]
which remains unseen. But we can return here to exercis[...]
discernment, allowing the eyes of our hearts to behold [...]
invisible. No man has seen God, but we have seen Ch[...]
(John 1:18; 14:7-11). The unseen may feel unbelievabl[...]
and it is on our own (1 Corinthians 2:9-10). Human e[...]
alone cannot see Jesus and believe (Mark 15:32; John 6:[...]
20:29). Faith requires an inward gaze upon the glory[...]
God. As Christ teaches, "Blessed are those who have
seen and yet have believed" (John 20:29).

Furthermore, given the world and its fallen, fail[...]
and frustrating state, it may feel difficult to become assu[...]
of the things we hope for, as Hebrews exhorts. Again,[...]
may feel personally inclined, even pressured by the w[...]
to push aside hope and remove it from the table of
experience. But faith requires it. Our very salvation i[...]
intertwined with hope, one is indistinguishable without [...]
other (Psalm 42:1; 43:5; 119:81, 166; Romans 5:2; 1 [...]
inthians 15:19; 1 Thessalonians 5:8).

We may think that hope is something intrinsic[...]
placed within us that slowly chips away as we witness
experience suffering, disappointment, and an assortmen[...]
other trials within the world. But we would be wrong. [...]

writes to the church in Rome, "Through [Christ] we have also obtained access by faith into this grace in which we stand, and we rejoice in hope of the glory of God. Not only that, but we rejoice in our sufferings, knowing that suffering produces endurance, and endurance produces character, and character produces hope, and hope does not put us to shame" (Romans 5:2-5).

It is not that hope should fade away because of our suffering. Instead, suffering is the very launching pad for our hope. Suffering, endurance, and character are the stepping-stones to cultivating a hope that utterly rejects the prospect of our future shame. We can hope in God because we have received His love through the Holy Spirit, a sweet foretaste of what is still to come (Psalm 34:8; Proverbs 13:12; Romans 5:5).

I well understand that rejoicing in suffering is easier said than done. But that is exactly why we have the Holy Spirit—to make this impossible work possible. He is the Guarantee that grants us peace which surpasses understanding (Philippians 4:7). Responding with hope in the face of difficult circumstances, pain, and heartache can only be done as we abide in the loving Vine of Christ. As with anything, we cannot do it without Him.

What do we hope for? To reiterate, I am not talking about some fabled magic genie or personal fantasyland. What are the things *in Christ* that we absolutely hope for?

For example, I have frequently met saints in the Lord who have told me their greatest desire in life. These beloved brothers and sisters aspire to one day hear Jesus say to them, "Well done, good and faithful servant" (Matthew 25:14-30; Luke 11:19-27). In other words, their hope aims to be faithful unto the Lord and what He asks them to do.

In response to this aim, I always declare, "It's done." Many will look at me baffled at first, perplexed as to how I can answer so confidently. I explain that these hopes are perfectly aligned to the will of God. The Lord has placed this hope in their hearts. If this is their heart's desire, the Lord has begun the work and will prove faithful to complete it (1 John 5:14-15). I am convinced of it.

No one needs to live a life in which they are worried about whether they meet a spiritual quota of servitude before they hear their King's commendation. God does not maintain a leaderboard of believers who are serving Him. We have been justified and saved because of the all-encompassing and fully finished work of Jesus. As we boast in the Lord alone, should we hope to receive recognition from Him, we will (2 Corinthians 10:17-18). Again, we should not seek to do the work for the commendation in and of itself—ultimately, Jesus is our Prize (Philippians 3:14). But we should all rest assured again in what the Son of God cried out at Calvary: "It is finished."

In those last fifteen minutes of *The Shawshank Redemption* that I rewound to watch repeatedly, Red narrates over the final images, "I find I'm so excited, I can barely sit still or hold a thought in my head. I think it's the excitement only a free man can feel, a free man at the start of a long journey whose conclusion is uncertain. I hope I can make it across the border. I hope to see my friend and shake his hand. I hope the Pacific is as blue as it has been in my dreams. I *hope*."

Like Red, we too should rediscover—or discover for the first time if required—hope. Only, our conclusion *is* certain. Through whatever suffering we must experience, whatever endurance we must maintain, and whatever character we must build, hope will not put us to shame (Romans 5:5).

A TWIST BEGINNING

W hile we are on the topic of endings, that's a fitting place for us to finish. Like the fourteenth-century proverb says, "All good things must come to an end."

Only there's a surprise in store for us. Twist endings are always welcome in storytelling, and it's no different from the story that God is authoring. While every other good thing does eventually end, the peculiar thing about Jesus is, there is no end. True, He is the Beginning and the End, but that is not because our story will draw to a close, the curtains will fall, and the theatre will go dark (1 Corinthians 15:12-28).

He continues, as will we. Our mortal life is just act one of the whole story being written. Yes, it is a crucial act. But where we might believe our story ends, it is just getting started. We don't need to wait until the end of our lives to realize that new beginning either. It has already begun.

Paul writes, "So we do not lose heart. Though our outer self is wasting away, our inner self is being renewed day by day" (2 Corinthians 4:16). Just a little later, the apostle more succinctly announces, "Therefore, if anyone is in Christ, he is a new creation. The old has passed away; behold, the new has come" (2 Corinthians 5:17). Let us each wave goodbye to the old. Actually, let's pack the old into its coffin, where it rightfully belongs.

It is King Jesus Himself, seated on the throne who roars, "Behold, I am making all things new... these words are trustworthy and true" (Revelation 21:5). All things. All! Us, our hearts, our plans, our ways, our everything. This is surprising enough to be remarkably good news which we can—and should—share with anyone who will hear it, believer and unbeliever alike. Our rejoicing in this truth should never cease or wane.

However, there remains one mystery which we will not be able to quite put our finger on for a while yet. Something is still hidden from plain sight which God intends to reveal as we encounter the completion of His plans in us. The Bible puts it like this: "We shall not all sleep, but we shall all be changed" (1 Corinthians 15:52). While we may understand that we are children of God, destined for the throne with Him, He has not yet fully revealed what we will become (1 John 3:1-2).

We see this play out in Christ's own resurrection. After He rose from the dead, Mary mistook Jesus for a gardener (John 20:11-18). Later, two disciples encountered Jesus on the road to Emmaus and did not recognize Him over the course of an entire day's journey (Luke 24:13-35). Then the eleven disciples thought they saw a ghost when they first encountered the pierced Christ (Luke 24:36-37). Even before His final ascension, after forty days of being with the apostles, some still doubted (Matthew 28:16-17).

How is it that some people could still doubt Jesus after His resurrection, standing right there in the midst of them? Because He had been changed. He looked *like* Jesus, but He didn't look *exactly* like the Jesus they had known before His death, burial, and resurrection.

This goes to show that a resurrected life does not necessarily look like we think it might. On the other side of resurrection, the wounds of crucifixion remain. Where piercing has been experienced, the holes can still be touched (Luke 24:39). In fact, it is from these very wounds that a resurrected life in Christ can minister healing to others (2 Corinthians 1:3-7). It is because we too have been bruised, pierced, and crucified with Christ that we can participate in His work in the church and the world.

People are hurting, and our hurts often help in the healing process that only Jesus can fully bring. Such suffering might come to us emotionally, mentally, physically, or even spiritually, but in Christ, pain will come. It's an unavoidable yet necessary part of God's plan, part of His method to further conform us to His likeness (Romans 8:29; Ephesians 4:20-24). He will not let a single speck of our suffering go to waste (Genesis 50:20).

All this is to illustrate, what remains in store for each one of us is not yet fully known. His plans for us are not wholly distinguishable still. But we can trust that they are good (Jeremiah 29:11). They look like a crucified life, yes, that is necessary (Romans 6:6; Galatians 2:20; 5:24; 6:14). But more importantly, His plans for us look like a new and abundant life lived by the very power of God. Our life is now made possible by the exact same life that the resurrected Jesus operates by in the heavenly realms. We live by, through, for, and unto the King of kings, the Lord of lords, the Name above every name. We can do nothing apart from Him, and most importantly, we don't have to. He reigns and abides inside us, just as we also abide in Him (John 6:56; 15:1-17). The fruit is already being produced because of Him, even if it's still not appearing as immediately or abundantly as we might hope.

Assured of this reality, there is no story, no plan, and no work in our lives that will have a finish as surprisingly magnificent as the one Jesus has in store for His followers. God will obliterate in blinding, dazzling glory every expectation we could possibly imagine, every goal we have tried to achieve, and every effort we have tried to take. Words fail me as I consider His plans. I am awestruck as I consider Him.

One night not too many years ago, I sat next to a fire with my best friend, Ben, and his older brother, Joel. Both of them are men I admire in their walks of faith, consistently demonstrating hearts given wholly unto the Lord and filled with the Holy Spirit. After briefly catching up and some casual conversation over the flames, our discussion veered toward the spiritual.

While on the topic, Joel shared that, on his way to meet us, he prayed specifically for and about me. "God, what are You doing with Jonathan? What are You up to through him? What are You multiplying with him? What are You…" Rapidly, Joel rattled off a recap of his eager prayer, repeatedly asking what work Jesus was currently doing in and through me.

Rather quickly, Joel was silenced with an answer. "Who cares about any of that? Jonathan loves Me."

The fire in front of me blurred with tears as the words came out of Joel's mouth. "Thank You, Lord," my voice whispered, cracking with the burning log as embers rose against the night sky in golden splendor. "Thank You."

Trusting that God plans to perfectly finish me and every one of His plans for me, I too am finished. Undone by His incomparable holiness, crushing glory, unconditional love, and astounding grace, I don't need to do anything more. That's my master plan. I just want Him. I just want Jesus.

May we all set aside every other thing so that Christ might become our only pursuit, forever and ever, amen. He will do the rest. In fact, as we patiently walk along these riverbanks of eternity, it's already done.

QUESTION

What is God's plan for me?

ANSWER

Completing.

READ

Philippians 1:6

REFLECT

- Do you believe that God cares about your plans? Where might your timelines need some Spirit-led adjustment?
- Where has the Lord proven faithful to you in your life? Where have you potentially misinterpreted promises from God in your life?
- Where is it that Jesus has not shown up how or when you expect? Are there any current circumstances that feel like day four?
- What are the things you hope for in Christ? What has not yet been seen, but you feel convinced of in faith?
- Where have you experienced Jesus making things new in your life? What do you want to experience Him finish in you?

EVERYTHING THAT THAT REMAINS

He's done. We're not.

EPILOGUE

"**P**endulums swing nasty." This was the exact phrase that came to mind as I sat in a room with other aspiring authors, listening to the testimony of a brother in Christ named Matthew. He shared how the Lord had long ago revealed his practice of using relationships with others to his professional advantage. Broken by the realization, Matthew found his behavior so detestable that he decided to never again do anything that resembled it, avoiding any efforts to sell or promote himself or his business again. But in making this swing to doing the exact opposite, he now realized that he had also set aside promoting the work God intended to effectively complete through him. Right there, Matthew decided to find a middle ground with the Lord. There was a new way forward waiting for him.

Everyone has done this at some point or another. Especially in spiritual circles. If we come from a more legalistic-leaning background, when we grasp grace, we may throw out the Bible's many commands to do anything resembling "work" whatsoever. If we are accustomed to a church experience that is intensely scripture-focused but lacks free expressions of the Holy Spirit, when we encounter the active presence of God, we may instead become obsessed with the Spirit and will often reduce scripture to a nominal part or afterthought of our ongoing lives with Christ.

But we serve a God of both-and, not either-or. As Frank Viola has pointed out in much of his authorship, especially *Insurgence*, the gospel of Jesus Christ is not one of legalism or libertinism, but of both Lordship and Liberty. Our God is simple and mysterious; full of truth and grace; the light of the world and surrounded by clouds of darkness; for the mature and inherited by those who become like children (2 Samuel 22:12; Psalm 97:2; Matthew 18:3; John 1:14; 8:12; Ephesians 3:1-6; 1 Corinthians 14:20; 2 Corinthians 11:3; Colossians 1:28). The paradoxes of God and His kingdom are endless.

So, here we now sit, confronted with the idea that every believer's job is to do nothing apart from Christ. With this new awareness, the temptation may arrive rather quickly to stop doing anything whatsoever. Our lives may quickly swing from busy, potentially good activity to quiet, inert complacency. Or, if we are not much of an A-type personality in the first place, perhaps we will use this book's ideas as our proof to keep sitting on the couch, watching TV, eating Doritos, mistaking our lazy practices for a true Christian calling.

But remember, resting in Christ is not paralysis. Holistically speaking, I have not argued that there is nothing to do—only that whatever we do should be done in consistent partnership with what Jesus is already doing. It is He who will finish the work, not us. In fact, it is Christ who needs to begin it in the first place, as that will be the exclusive way any of our work might last.

This is a timeless message, but also one that I believe is very timely given the age (1 Chronicles 12:32). Everything—and everyone—is moving so fast today. But this is not leading us to deeper Christian understanding or experiences. It is keeping us shallow, ultimately "led astray from the simplicity and purity of devotion to Christ" (2 Corinthians 11:3, NASB).

While a healthy detox period from our doing may be required, as it was in my own experience, this should not remain our way of living indefinitely. In fact, it is even in this restful, slower pace of life in Christ that I have personally realized the greatest personal productivity ever, coworking with the Lord to accomplish work that I believe will prove quite lasting. This book is just one example. I cannot overstate the paramount truth that God works tirelessly while we sit, wait, and rest in Him.

Even having said all of this, I am certain this book will be misquoted, misrepresented, misheard, and misunderstood—and probably by people who haven't read anything more than the title. That's okay, I understand. I suspect that I would have combatted such ideas in my previous overdoing habits, too. Jesus has been irrefutably patient with me.

Whatever the outcome, I simply hope that this work serves the Lord's purposes, encouraging every one of my fellow saints to take heart, be still, and know that He is God (Psalm 46:10). He has things fully under control. We can relax, slow down, stop trying to make something big happen, and watch as He works in us. However long the Lord may have us each pause, eventually, we should all look up with spiritual eyes to answer, "What is Jesus doing?" He invites us to do it with Him, much to our continued befuddlement and His purpose's fulfillment.

As nasty as our pendulums may swing, He wants to help us swing back, slowly but surely finding the cool rhythm of a sustainable, always-empowered life in His Spirit. Jesus reminds us even now, "apart from Me, you can do nothing." But give it a little while, and He always continues, "Let's go." God has a plan.

STUDY GUIDES AND OTHER EXTRAS

To learn more about this book and engage further with its ideas, please visit ICanDoNothing.com. Extras include:

- **Detox for Doers**, a devotional that will help people "strive to enter that rest" (Hebrews 10:23). Start working at not working.
- **Do Nothing Together**, an interactive small group study based on the lessons and chapters of this book. Begin walking—not running—with others in the Christian community.
- **A behind-the-book interview**, where author Jonathan Cottrell shares more about this book, the story behind it, and what doing nothing looks like in his own life.

- **I Can Do Nothing**, a worship song sheet and audio file, with lyrics written by Jonathan Cottrell and music composed by Gregory Kyle Klug, for license-free use in any church meeting.
- **#WIJD** bracelets, screensavers, and other paraphernalia that finally ask the more valuable question. Encourage the right trend.

ACKNOWLEDGMENTS

I have so many to thank. I will probably ramble on a bit too long here, but the backs of books are rarely meant for every reader. I can't publish this without acknowledging, in writing, the people who have helped shape me, this work, and its contents.

First, I must thank my incredible wife, Nicole Cottrell. I am indebted to your love and thankful to Jesus every day for gifting me with you. Without your undying support in everything I have done, not to mention your wisdom and grace in helping build me up, this book would simply not exist. Nor would our incredible children, without each of whom my life would be less full of joy to experience, learning to gain, and stories to tell.

Riley, Tolan, and Beckett, you have each changed me for the better and taught me more about the Father than I could ever otherwise know. It is my daily privilege to be your dad.

Geoffrey Gentry, though I have not known you long, I am incredibly grateful for your effort in helping keep me accountable and guiding my edits while writing. This is a far better book as a result. Moreover, I have gained a true friend in the process.

Mom and Dad, you taught me better than I could have asked for. But more importantly, thank you for loving me better than I could have asked for. It is my esteemed honor to be your son, and I hold you in the highest of regards. Your legacy will last forever.

Were it not enough that I have learned what it means to meet under the headship of Jesus alongside my church family, each and every one of them has played some role in encouraging, equipping, and edifying me over many years, too. I cannot overlook them. Juice, Evan, Greg, (Dr.) Renee, John, Taylor, Joseph, Holly, Tim, Jeanette, Devin, Ashleigh, John, Debbie, Shawn, Jodi, Chad, Chris, Senta, Mike, Sydney, Eric, Sheila, Steve, Jana, Keith, Alexis, Phil, Randi, David, Renee, and the whole, beautiful lot of you near and far—what a gift it is to be your brother.

Ben Forsberg, thank you for being my best friend and letting me be yours. Thank you for encouraging me to write this, too, knowing it resonated with both of our results-oriented natures. Thank God for His grace in teaching us what it means to do nothing.

David, thank you for being my brother and putting up with me in our youth. I need you. And Sarah, my lovely sister, thank you for joining our wild family, expanding my heart's space for those three little giants, Claire, Cole, and Caleb.

Mary, my amazing aunt—and friend—I am thankful for you and the health you helped me rediscover. Not to mention many trips to Disney World.

To the men who have poured into me as spiritual fathers and wise mentors, I am ridiculously grateful for and stronger because of your imprints upon my life. Kevin Youngblood, Bruce Everette, Brian Farone, Doug Scott, Jeff Goble, Rick Schmitz, and you many others who have participated in modeling Jesus for me, thank you, thank you, thank you.

Men of the morning meetings, Jesus is stirring something in Phoenix. Thank you for your faithful prayers, reminding me that these pages were already written in God's eyes. You were right, here they are.

Frank Viola, your ministry has had greater direct and indirect effect on me than any other, without parallel or comparison. Your faithful and humble service unto the Lord astounds me, and I have gained fresh insight into and passion for the eternal purpose of God because of you and your palpable love for Jesus. Further, Scribe was but one other catalyst in this book being realized as quickly as it was. I cannot thank you enough for your personal impact on me, for introducing me to many of the authors I have quoted in this very book, or for the Deeper Christian Life ministry that is an undeniably visible testimony of Jesus Christ on the Earth.

Watchman Nee, I cannot wait to meet and embrace you, the alabaster jar that taught me what brokenness truly means. Brennan Manning, you helped me more fully grasp a grace that truly is amazing. A.W. Tozer, you furthered pursuit in me. Dietrich Bonhoeffer, our life together awaits. Brother Lawrence, I am eager to enjoy the Presence with you. Bob Goff, you get Love. And Mary DeMuth, it is *Everything* which helped me find the tone for *Nothing*. Imagine, that. Only, your words are more elegant; I aspire.

To the rest of my family, friends, collaborators, influencers, and the like, nothing can cease my effusive thanks for you. I hope everyone stays for my story's credits (jonathancottrell.com/credits), because I can't imagine my life story without any of you. Behold, the pages and gratitude of an exuberantly rich man.

Finally, foremost of all, I thank Jesus Christ, the Holy Spirit, and Abba Father, my one Master who is constantly working in and on me, always patient, ever kind, and well beyond the paltry description I stammer and stutter in sight of Him.

You are Everything, Lord. Please have mine.

ABOUT THE AUTHOR

My name is Jonathan Cottrell, and I'm a recovering doer. I hope to avoid writing about all—or any—of my work here. That would partially defeat the point of what I have written in this book. If you wish to walk alongside me as I seek to follow Jesus, I can be found online at JonathanCottrell.com. So long as I am alive and available, I invite anyone to call or text me at (480) 319-0448, too. After all, I'm no more accomplished in Christ than any other believer. Better yet, we're family.

A free ebook edition is available with the purchase of this book.

To claim your free ebook edition:

1. Visit MorganJamesBOGO.com
2. Sign your name CLEARLY in the space
3. Complete the form and submit a photo of the entire copyright page
4. You or your friend can download the ebook to your preferred device

A **FREE** ebook edition is available for you or a friend with the purchase of this print book.

CLEARLY SIGN YOUR NAME ABOVE

Instructions to claim your free ebook edition:
1. Visit MorganJamesBOGO.com
2. Sign your name CLEARLY in the space above
3. Complete the form and submit a photo of this entire page
4. You or your friend can download the ebook to your preferred device

Print & Digital Together Forever.

Snap a photo   Free ebook   Read anywhere